THE MANASA SAROVAR

Itty 'O (Itty Oommen)

Clever Fox® PUBLISHING
Chennai • Bangalore

CLEVER FOX PUBLISHING
Chennai, India

Published by CLEVER FOX PUBLISHING 2025

ISBN: 978-93-6707-791-7

Behold, I stand in the hush of bewilderment,
At the mystery Thy hand hath wrought.
Low does my brow descend,
Kissing the dust that drank the footsteps of Thy will.
From the hollow vessel of my clay-born frame
Rises a hunger not of bread but of utterance—
To pour the secret gratitude of my depths
For the gift of joy Thou hast poured like living waters
Into this unworthy jar of clay.
And lo, by Thy mercy,
My tongue is loosed to carve humble syllables,
That they may carry a shadow of Thy truth.

Itty 'O

AUTHOR'S PROLOGUE

I know not the craft of words,
Nor the art of speech,
Yet from some hidden spring,
Thy praise spilt through my hand.

For joys and wounds alike, I bow;
Still I thirst, for Thy play the endless.
Seeds once buried in forgotten pages
Now bloom with a quiet light.

Graced by the gentle urgings from many,
I was kept on the path when I would stray.
These verses rise from moments true—
From nature's touch, from skies unknown.

Small I stand, before the peaks of knowledge;
Where I falter, let this be my apology.
I leave these lines to those who seek,
While I wait in the green room,
Longing for the next call to the stage.

Itty 'O, October 2025

CONTENTS

1

The Sleep

Sometimes Thy shine wakes my soul,
In midnight's hush, serene and whole;
My eyelids close in a reflex deep,
Yet still, the mind will not let me sleep.

The greedy thoughts their snares prepare,
With rows of plans laid out with care;
And while I toss in the restless fight,
My body bends to my mind's own might.

Yet wakefulness, with tender grace,
Opens the heart to Thy embrace;
I thank the days, the trials, and the cheer,
And drink the calm that lingers near.

Like cattle chewing meadow's green store,
I taste the gifts of my life once more;
Till in nameless light my spirit sways,
And the dream's soft hand leads me away.

From dawn to dusk, the mind will chase,
It's shadowed prey through time and space;
It weaves its nets to pull me down,
And wears the night as a selfish crown.

But like silver scars in midnight's dome,
Telling winds they've passed, and peace hast come;
Thy eternal power fills each cell,
Where grasping mind dares not to dwell.

Thy radiance floods this earthly frame,
And calls me toward the formless name;
It feeds with rich, unmeasured silence,
Where all is pure, and every vision serene.

So draw me close, O' Lord of light,
To serve with all the gifted, the inward might;
Send again the lightning signs, to stir my soul,
Till I lay in Thee at the end, fully and whole.

Awaken me from life's dream-bound stay,
To walk in the nature's natural way;
To join Thy play beneath the sun,
Aware of myself, while many others run.

2

Hymn of the Nature

O' Lord, let this dainty soul draw near,
To bow before Thy shrine in prayer;
Those ancient scripts declare with light-
That meditative hearts may find the sight.

Lead me to paths unknown, untold,
Where prayers are whispered, pure and bold;
Till every playful breath, I make to live-
A note that melts through all I live.

How can Thy might in words be bound,
Or even trillions can hold that sound?
Teach me the silence vast and deep-
Where truth awakens for all alive.

Time gave me names from the ages past,
Yet none could hold Thy truth at last;
So guide me, O' Lord, that I may stay-
In step with Thy eternal play.

I hear Thy hymn in the morning breeze,
In stars that burn above the seas;
In birds, those chant, in trees those dance-
In all the waves that rise as if in a trance.

Yet here I stand, unsure, ashamed,
A wanderer who seeks Thy name;
Still longing, O' Lord, for Thee to show-
The way where silent rivers flow.

When the mind is restless, and the body weak,
Thy word becomes the truth I seek;
And hurdles fade like passing breath-
Before the doors of life and death.

O' whisper once Thy cosmic law,
That leaves my soul in a holy awe;
Where love is all, and myself is none-
And every heart beats into One.

When innocence and prayer unite,
Existence works its hidden rite;
As a speck of dust, I rise to Thee-
A droplet joins Thy boundless sea.

In hollow peace, in formless grace,
I see Thy shine in every place;
Till my self is scattered as mist to ray-
Absorbed within Thy boundless play.

3

Who Am I

Amazing nature, bright with wonder,
Clothing the earth in a living art;
Seasons wheel in ceaseless thunder,
Yet each ends where new ones start.

Trees lift their arms to greet the heavens,
Grass stays low, yet serene, and complete;
None compares nor competes for the given,
All life in harmony, keeping the beat.

In their stillness dwells a treasure,
Freed from the mind's unending game;
Their silent hymns, too vast to measure,
They rise to praise Thy holy name.

Moonlit skies in jewelled splendour,
Whisper truths the mortal heart can not hear;
Though the shrine may stand in grandeur,
Still, my soul feels far, and not near.

Life's wide ocean holds me drifting,
Waves at war on every side;
Few like eagles soar uplifting,
Few in silent depths they abide.

Shadows grow when light draws near,
False, yet born of a radiance true;
All creation moves in an unseen honour,
Why must human hearts undo the same?

Wake my senses up or down, to find my way,
The paths still bright, yet never trod;
Lead me where Thy truth shall arise,
Draw me deep into Thy core.

When the soul hears heaven's sighing,
All illusions fade and cease, to bind;
Wisdom falls through a silence, underlying,
As soft as snow on tranquil minds.

Let me cross that border slender,
Stretch my soul to reach Thy domain;
End my wandering, make me render,
A life in tune with nature's terrain.

4

This Earthen Fiddle

Thou hast shaped this earthen fiddle,
Formed to sound Thy sacred will;
In testing notes, both strong and brittle,
Guiding my hands through good and ill.

Yet this fiddle feels its binding,
Trained to stay in mortal bands;
Playing songs, the brain designing,
Not the ones Thy heart commands.

When it hums in highs and lows,
In a sacred rhythm deep and wide,
Wisdom blooms like secret flowers,
Fed by grace from every side.

As a child, I took each measure,
To grasp every tune without debate;
Till the world in fleeting pleasure,
Dimmed the light that shone innate.

Still, the bow must meet the stringing,
Play the notes Thy will hast spun;
Soft or loud, the echoes ringing,
Where all are fair beneath the sun.

Desires may spin in tiny circles,
Like a fly so swift in the restless air;
Still, the bird ascends in hidden marvels,
Unbound, though no reward is near.

When Thy grace flows free and slender,
Joining the freedom's silent dance,
All the tones grow pure and tender,
In Thy boundless, and bright expanse.

Thus, the soul finds the true releasing,
Blends with light, no night can dim;
Every bow-stroke, sweet yet ceasing,
But moves in endless praise to Thee.

5

This World, a Paradise

This world, a paradise, a gift from the hands of the Divine;
A finely crafted home for all, a treasure truly mine.

The soil has fed through ages, all,
The air gives breath each moment to all;
The sun and stars shine equally,
To light every living way,
The planet's gifts are unending,
Its beauty pure and wide in shine,
Enough for generations yet to come,
Certainly enough for all to bide.

Why fear the apocalypse or counting time,
When our life is here left to live?
The skies and seas, the hills and plains,
Have plenty more than what they gave,
And each moment holds a blissful embrace,
And each breath a chance to sense;
The joy of sharing the earth with all—
Brings peace that belongs to all.

Yet men divide the world with flag and wall,
And draws the lines that may claim all;
From nations down to families or groups,
Each builds a smaller name in the shades,
But truth is never shaded nor bounded,
Nor love by fences chained or crossed;
The centre of existence calls—
And none are ever lost in the call.

It's the ego that births the wars of man,
And crowns them all as clowns, unseen;
While the needs and hunger lie ignored,
Man feeds his pride and lust in the dark,
But still the earth keeps the spinning,
The stars are still brightly burning;
And peace awaits the soul that knows—
To love all with no expectations.

O' Lord, let the veils be lifted away,
Let all the shadows fade away;
The golden glow within shall rise,
And guide each to the day, where all rise.
Where war and hatred are buried deep,
And selfishness long extinct in a weep,
The truth will shine and all will sing—
This world a paradise, a gift from the hands of the Divine;
A finely crafted home for all, a treasure truly mine.

6

The Mystical Stream And Its Ferry

There flows a stream in mystic gleam, its ferry swift and kind,
It bear the newborns, purity in a bliss, from realms all have left behind;
To blue-clad worlds at dawn's first breath, as it sails through the silver skies,
Yet none recall the hidden shores where first we opened our eyes.
Perhaps a silence guards the old, perhaps some veils hide the past,
While innocence and the living light kept glowing deep inside so fast.

In childhood's days, all caught faint strains, a whisper through the air,
Where laughter wove with tender ache, and wonder lingered around there;
The peace of the eternal tide was calling all soft and still,
But we knew not its secret paths, nor yet Thy own will.
Yet faintly shone a guiding flame, through the shadows

dim and long,
A hush that stirred within the heart, and woke from far an unknown song.

We reached this shore all bare but crowned, with a spirit bright and free,
By loving hands were sheltered close, in folly's own gaiety setting us free;
Through gentle fields or rugged roads, the shifting seasons passed along,
And we, through gains and losses unalike, saw nothing meant for us to last,
Until the sun in noonday blaze shone full upon our own brow,
And time, once slow, was racing fast, though we scarce knew it how.

We felt not yet the growing weight of all the treasures we had sought,
The burden of the drowsy race, whose rest is dearly set and bought;
We chased delights, and pleasures rare, and strove for illusive names,
But lost the song our hearts once played, forgot from whence we came.
And the return ferry and the shiny stream, the journey yet to be,
Lay far towards the reach of those who grasp the world too greedily.

The evening came with a sudden rush, the horizon bathed in gold unstained,
We counted walls of trophies high, and measured what we'd gained;
Yet there the waiting ferry stood—no plea could hold it slow or still,
The body went bent, the mind grew tired and whispered the Heaven's will,
The river's hush called hearts to rest, beyond the striving life on this shore,
Where silent stars inscribed the truth: the gathered gains are not thine anymore.

And when the dark enfolds the tide, the soul may yet return bare,
As pure as when it first set forth, a lesson truly learned when aware;
But some, though rich in outward store, find the spirit cold and pale,
And drift to realms incongruous, still burdened by their care,
Yet those unstained shall meet the Whole, in a formless decree,
A drop dissolved forevermore within the boundless sea of Thee.

7

The Doorway Home

I set my feet upon the road unbound by years,
A path unseen by the mortal eyes,
Without the first step, without the last mile,
Where suns have risen and faded without any count,
And skies have folded over the worlds left uncounted.

The soul remembers where all shall care,
Yet the cloak of earth clings on our shoulders,
Bidding all to linger upon its shore,
To taste its joys, to drink its sorrows,
To learn the weight of passing days.

But a stirring awoke within the depths,
A voice not born of breath nor tongue,
A whisper that broke the stillness of ages,
And an unseen hand lead the real me,
Over waters no boat has ever sailed,
Over lands no traveller has ever claimed,
Away from the dust and the weight of life,
Into a freedom my heart had never known.

The Eternal weaves the thread of unseen time ahead,
Through the hidden looms of time ahead,

While I, sit in the dark shadow of today,
Bind tomorrows with the seen cords of yesterday,
Yet neither tide nor time shall wait,
And the call grew louder until it became my breath.

Within this earthen vessel burns a hidden flame,
Silent, pure, unbroken from the very first shine,
I wrapped it in the robes of pride and longing,
And forgot it complete, even in my own keeping,
But now I sense the lost key was always mine,
Pressed into my palm before the dawn.

As the seed aches for the sun,
As the hornbill longs to devour the spring,
So does my soul ache to lift all the masks,
To let the truth pour in like a dawn unseen,
To rise unbroken, with a heart so sacred,
And set my course for the radiant shore.

No lightning shall unseat my steps,
No thunder shall drown the song within,
Neither praise nor shame shall chain my feet,
Nor any shadow's shape divert my eyes,
For I am bound for the land beyond all the stars,
Where joy needs no measure nor shining,
And the light knows no darkness nor dimming.

The key lies in every heart,
The sooner turned, all sooner home.
All trials, all treasures, and it's pains,
Are but the soft weighing of pale spirits,

Until the balance tips into an emptiness,
The soul flies swifter than the light itself.

Forgive my faltering in the dust,
Forgive the days I closed my eyes,
When the death comes as it surely will,
I shall not turn, I shall not hide,
But greet the shadow with a smile,
For it is but the doorway Home.

8

Losing Myself

I was losing my Self, piece by piece,
While striving hard for many, to comfort and please;
I traded my shine for respect, pride and gold,
For name and for fame, for the stories they told.

I followed the crowd, through smile and through cry,
In charity's masks, where the truth went awry;
Bound in the chains that they called "duty's way,"
While deep in my heart, a Dawn was stirring the day.

They counted it as virtues, as noble and right,
Yet anchored my being away from the light;
But under the surface, a radiance burned,
A spark for its limitless Source that it yearned.

To walk in the rhythm creation had spun,
To work with perfection as the two become one;
To act without striving, yet all to be fresh and true,
In the unseen excellence that comes into view.

In the end lost all the world, but my Self I did find,
While some only laughed, and some stayed behind;
A few felt the tremor and knew what it meant,
While most slept in the shadows where light never went.

Yet silence remained as a luminous guide,
Yet emptiness glowed with the cosmos inside;
Yet the formless spark held its shimmering thread,
While the aura of galaxies capped all that was said.

This is my journey, my vow and my chance,
To find my own Self, not to lose it to any name or fame;
Through all I release, through all I let go,
I gather the truth, perhaps the seekers may know.

9

Wisdom, The Boundless Feel

From outer worlds, all the texts are drawn,
Woven by the hands of man, in soft comforts spawn,
Yet wisdom's flame not taught and sought,
Yet it blooms within, from where the stars reside,
From the core where all the beginnings rise,
Beneath the untold veil of mortal mists.

In sacred emptiness, the child returns,
Innocence reigns, and wonder burns,
The hidden key turns, silent but sure,
And opens gates to wisdom so pure.

Trust the lantern to guide the way,
But clouds of shadows dim its ray;
Words went twisted, with the tiny power gained,
And gold in greedy palms remained,
And springs of truth were blindfolded tight,
Lost to the endless sleep of the night.

Where now is love seen? Where now is peace for sense?
When shall the passions wake and hatreds cease?

Greed and rivalry roam the land; instead,
Ego rules all minds, and with every hand,
While weary men in slumber stay,
Dreaming their fading lives away.

Knowledge without awareness drains,
Like honey spilled on barren plains;
Yet knowledge joined in insight's gleam,
Becomes the Sun's eternal beam,
A silent knock on the heaven's door,
Revealing love that needs nothing no more,
And peace so vast, no name can bind,
A boundless home for all mankind.

10

The Sun and the Moon

O' the Unseen, who hast gifted sun and moon,
Shining daily, night and noon,
The radiance flowing, the love unending,
Life and breath to all things lending.

Candles burn, yet none can be,
The sun's bright ray of majesty;
Moonlight strives strong in silver grace,
In reflections, but not Thy golden face.

Countless creeds in numberless names,
Seeking peace through mirrored flames,
Yet all their lights, combined as one,
Match not the glory of the ray of Thy sun.

We chase illusions, in fleeting vain,
Build castles so proud on the sand's domain,
Racing away from the rays of holy light,
In masks unknown, wandering in the night.

O' sun and moon, the resolute pair,
Shine and shine to wake our souls till free,
Lead us past all the desires' snare,
Towards the realms divine, beyond compare.

11

The Unfathomable Wonder

Since time began, mankind has sought,
Through the temple's wall and sacred thought,
With drum and deed, with chant and flame,
Perhaps all are shadows of the same,
They plead for favours from the skies,
For blessings bright, for gracious sighs;
But flowers, gold, and songs are small,
If not, the self is given in full.

They walk the path of seasoned rites,
They seek the eternal starry heights,
They hope their whispered prayers ascend,
Yet keep the heart, they will not spend.
But if the unfathomable miracle may once fall,
And grace an eternal flood for all,
Thy breath, Thy light, Thy boundless ray,
Would pierce this clay in which I stay.

When colours whirl through mind's vast stores,
Where all the vessels rise with hopes;
Yet none could match that touch of Thine,
That melts own heart for wonders unseen.
And if the vessel cracks, then let it break!

For in Thy aura, that is all I take;
And if my soul survives the fire,
It shall but voice thy sole desire.

"Let wars be still, let hatred cease,
Let earth be crowned with Thy holy peace;
Let love pour forth through every seam,
Restore the first- ever - born dream;
Make all as one, a star born band,
Where truth is the tongue on every land."

Let egos fade, let pride lie down,
Let mercy wear the royal crown;
Let Earth become another shining dome,
Where every soul hast found its home.
Let's dissolve into that so great song,
That moves the wheeling stars all along.

And if time's sands still within its downward stream,
Then bless the dear ones in a dream;
Let joy be sown and pain kept afar,
Or better, share all things that are all around.
Yet, in Thy play, we stand at last,
The earthen jar by time's overcast;
And rest within a bliss profound,
Where end is none, where none is found.

12

Two Shadows

Two shadows follow all, silent but near,
At dawn or dusk, they still appear,
One hides where midnight's corners creep,
One walks in light, yet stays in a silent sleep.
The shadow of death, as dreamers feared,
The shadow of truth, as the waking jeered.

Illusions flare like sparks to flame,
Or drift as smog to dim the name,
Of Light that calls beyond the mind,
While chains of delusions still unwind,
A fleeting vision, soft and sly,
All crown as life, yet fear to die.

Yet Thou art present on all so near,
Through thorn and stone, through doubt and fear.
Though trials that pierce, Thy love sustains,
No soul is lost, no hope remains in chains.
Through raging waves and restless tides,
For sure, all shall sense Thy grace that guides.

So mark the shadows, for false and true,
And walk in wisdom, clear of view.

Move within the play the Heavens weave,
In tune with all that we see and sense.
Bow for the joy, bow for the pain,
For death's no loss, but home again,
For the wise, a final step, serene and sure,
Into the arms of Truth, most pure and sure.

13

A Colloquy With the Mind

I wandered long in a restless chase,
The mind's wide window as my place;
Like one who hunts his shadow's hue,
Through halls of thought I ever flew.
Its whispers sweet as honey's stream,
It's lures unbroken like a dream;
Since the tree of knowing grew,
All served its will, yet knew not true.

I bowed before its reasoning throne,
And missed the Truth that softly shone;
I poured my trust in visions vain,
And drifted far from the peaceful plain.
I worshipped ego's golden face,
The hidden tyrant's cold embrace;
It cast a mirage on the boundless sky,
Too bright for any servant to deny.

From it arose the seeds of strife,
That choked the love and peace within my life;
Anguish, anger, and selfish gain,
Hatred's fire in thought's domain.

It veiled my sight in a fettered mind,
Promising greener pastures undefined;
Yet all dissolved in the burning sand,
When Silence called with an empty hand.

Thy holy Emptiness still waits,
Beyond the seen self, beyond all unseen gates;
To dwell therein is to be crowned,
Where only Thy pure light is found.
For I, a spark of boundless flame,
Am drawn to Thee from whence I came;
Thy love, unmeasured, and ever flows,
Through age on age all spirit knows,
It draws me home through night's long pine,
It draws me to Thy endless shrine.

14

A Confluence With the Soul

I slept as one in stories so old,
Like a Rip Van Winkle, lost and cold,
Till lightning's whisper split the night,
And music stirred my soul into light.
Yet walls of barter, walls of pride,
Rose high within my mind to hide;
They kept the truth so far away,
And left my path in deep decay.

When awoke, the world was so strange, in chains,
The warmth of heart weighed down by unseen chains;
Thick smog and shadow choked the air,
The ego's schemes, highly bred there.
Fern and ivy claimed the way,
And silent signs hidden from the day;
Through dreams of green I lay in sleep,
Where numerous calls could never seep.

Yet now a song through all resounds,
In every sky or cloud, on every ground;

I had been deaf and dumb, but now I hear,
I cleanse the dust, I drew the light near.
Illusion's reign must end in death,
It's barriers choke the soul's own breath;
They hide the gate to realms divine,
Where all the shining kingdoms shine.

And lo, the dust dissolves into the air,
The plans of joy and pain grow bare;
Like from fairy tales to truth returned,
Like diamond flames through worlds that burned.
So pure, so bright, not seen before,
I step within the timeless door;
In silence now my speech is heard,
And I hear Thy everlasting word.

And there, within the cosmic play,
I lose myself and cease to stray;
The self dissolves, the heart takes wings,
And joins the song that true spirit sings.

15

Thy Temple

O peerless shrine, that crowns all heights,
Outshining all man's work and mights,
No proof for the wise, nor need to seek,
Thy name all ancient epics speak.

This wondrous form that breathes and lives,
Bears the seal of love Thy mercy gifts;
Yet mankind dims the compassion's flame,
And stains the temple to self's acclaim.

They build bright, tall towers of stone and gold,
In glitter's trust, in wealth's strong hold;
Yet Thy true shrine, serene and near,
Lies veiled to the eyes that dream in fear.

O' the tiny star supreme, so still, so near,
Draw us from the fields grown cold and sere,
From faiths for wars, from a restless mind,
Into the circle and to the Center, pure and refined.

For purity is born gifted within,
Where souls feel where the deep pulses begin;
Through paths of many names and ways,
Lead us to truth's eternal rays,
Where only the unchanged truth remains.

16

From Emanation To Play

From the emanation's secret start,
I journey forth with a seeking heart;
Yet no footprints mark the veiled terrain,
While dust and smog obscure the plain.
Yet from the depths a spark takes flame,
A steady star without any name;
It draws me past my self's own snare,
And lifts me to Thy cosmic fair.

Where rills that weave through vale and glade,
They tame the stones, for halting the path made;
Though banks may bind their crystal streams,
Within its stillness, swells the force of eternal dreams.
So is the soul, when pressed and chained,
Conceals the power it has gained;
And if not freed by a tender hand,
Will burst all walls at Thy command.

The seasons pass with gentle tread,
And scatter leaves of dry and gold;
The buds give way to summer's leaves
Which autumn curls, which winter grieves.

Fear not the fading of thy frame,
Nor mourn the image, mask, nor name;
These garments fray, these shadows fall—
They are but dreams, and dreams so small to fall.

Feel neither the dark, nor blaze the light,
Know neither loss, nor gain in sight;
Hear not the drums of dancing days,
But only nature's endless praise.
Its scent and song no tongue can bind,
They touch the stars and flood the mind;
Taste not of envy's bitter waves,
When in the cosmic tides all lave.

This is the play, both vast and near,
The simplest truth, yet hard to clear;
For those who not come unto the core,
Must leave themselves outside its door.
And there, within that centre bright,
No self remains, no shade, no night;
But only silence, beyond all clay can supply—
A heart forever in Thy play.

17

Tears of a Planet

The aching grief of Mother Earth's tears,
Sharpens my heart—to heed the silent fears;
To turn from the glitter, the passing charm,
And to listen well to the wind's low psalm,
Where sorrow hides 'neath darkened skies,
And thunder speaks in muffled cries.
Once the earth wore robes of azure bright,
Feeding the children in endless delight;

Now scarred by shadows, and falsehood's stain,
A sacred play, disturbed by man for pain;
The breath grown shallow, the spirit worn,
The robe of a guardianship strongly torn.
The mourning sky still weeps above,
Once free, once vivid, a wanderer of love;
Pouring life in rains, unmeasured and free,
Now in whispering wounds no eye can see.

The sun still strides in timeless grace,
Yet burns with a sharper, harsher face;
Glaciers murmur of melting years,
Also, ice caps weep in retreating tears.
Test not the patience of the eternal unseen,

Prepare a path for the ages to appear;
What once was a pastime, careless and small,
Now poisons the breath that sustains us all.

Innovations cloaked in the clever's name,
Yet rooted in smoke, decay, and flame;
O' world, bow low to the womb that bore,
Lay down the arrogance of gun and war.
For war is the language of ruin's raw tongue,
Pouring venom where fresh rivers are meant to run;
Still all eyes turn toward their petty schemes,
While the wound grows wide beyond all dreams.

They march for flags on a fleeting land,
For borders drawn by the mortal hand;
They speak of peace with a sharpened blade,
Yet peace retreats where their cannons fade.
No victor ever stood on a field of graves,
For all are bound as the war-ship's slaves;
The earth bears scars from previous prideful claim,
While Heavens weep in an endless shame.

Now is the moment to stand awake,
To feel earth's grief for existence's sake.
Unite to hear the cry before
It falls into a silence forevermore.
If love feels lost, then unbar the gate,
Be still to know Thy truth's own weight;
And Existence shall plant a holy hand
A dawn of peace to heal the land.

Else this planet, once in truthful grace,
Shall lie in ashes, as a forsaken place;
Thy play disturbed, Thy breath denied,
The living scattered, the unborn defied.
So rise, O' soul, though small it seems,
And stand with the planet in purest dreams;
Guard the cradle, the sky, the sea, and the plants,
For truth, for peace of life, and for Thy eternal love.

18

Luck or Destiny

Loafing by the still backwaters, I beheld a scene in living grace,
An egret bathing in the last golden rays of the day,
While drizzles descended like silver threads from heaven,
As the world swiftly wore its evening crown.

The bird sought one last morsel before the sun withdrew,
Unmoved by the glowing sky, unfazed by the horizon's fire below,
The waves danced as golden anklets, the wind hummed its closing hymns,
Yet the gaze pierced only the rippling depths.

The bird preened the wings as if anointing for a flight,
Perhaps to greet the rain's arrival, or to return to her kin,
And in a swift dive and back, a silver captive in her beak,
A life struggling against life, in a moment's clasp.

But haste betrayed the bird as the fish slipped free,
Back into the cool embrace of the water's womb beneath,

The bird stood in a shadow of its own surprise,
One termed as joy, gone yet one freedom born.

What says the lake? What whispers the dusk?
That gain and loss are but a single turning,
That joy and sorrow spring from the same hidden source,
That destiny and luck drink from the same eternal
stream.

19

Sparks From The Desert

O' wanderer of the ages, tracing steps upon shifting sands,
Your path knows no map; the whisper of the wind, the compass.
Each grain beneath thy feet tells the stories of those gone before,
And each horizon thou chase dissolves into another - endless and new.

The sun walks beside thee by day, a beloved golden companion,
The moon follows thou by night, misty and milky, yet in a watchful vision,
And stars spill their blessings in many unseen secret patterns,
A guiding without commands, a teaching without words.

O' mirage of the golden flames in the heat unwind,
A puzzle for the newborn, as you treat the stranger who travels,
Shimmering in the scorching heat, may be a palace for the mind.

Yet once the bitter truth is tasted, an awareness take its roots,
No more shall the wise chase thee,
And when you rise again in the distance to fool,
The wise filters the real from the unreal,
Gift of the desert's warm lesson.

Perhaps you drink from the well of solitude, cool and deep,
And dine upon the bread of patience, baked in the furnace of trials.
The storms of sand that rise against you, fierce and blinding,
Yet only cleanse thy insight until the way is clear again.

O' wind that scatters the sand mounds in tiny pieces,
You swirl countless grains into the blinding walls,
Testing the sight and the spirit of those who walk the dunes,
Whereas in the cities far away, where sand makes no traces,
But fancies and lusts arise, alluring and bright,
To mask all vision, blindfolding the truth.
Yet when wisdom shines, all illusions shall fall,
For the divine play is seen from afar as tall.

O' the pilgrim soul, not bound by place nor season,
Carry within you the sanctuary no tempest can breach,
For the journey itself is a shrine, and the road the prayer,
And the end of this life for all in a wishful quench,
Is but the door to another dawn, if in prayer.

20

When the Mist Lifts, the Light Remains

Like a lush green tree, dense in thoughts,
We bar the sun, inviting our own darkness.
We trust the fading greens that surround us,
Believing the wither to be the eternal lights.

Dense veils of illusion coil around all, dimming the sacred glow,
Mists of mind prevail, guarding the gate to the inner shrine.
Where the salient power within lies ignored,
The slumbering life drifts in the bindings of its own blindness.

Yet life, what all see is believing the glitters around,
Mistaking the shadows or reflections for the light.
And we stretch our days in vain's pursuits,
Burdened with struggles, born of shaded fears.

Only when the leaves all fall, we see the sky,
Like the mist melts beneath the morning sun.
Then the shine returns unbidden, in its wisdom,
And the mist fades for nothing, leaving a sky of peace,
Vast, unbroken, and a truth so real.

21

An Ancient Ledger

Ancient barter in healthy breaths, in shadowed ways,
From nations' halls to the heart's dim maze;
It moves unseen, yet its roots run deep,
In love's disguise, where all the jealousies sleep.

Gifts without love wear an affection's mask,
Yet bind the souls to an unholy task;
Silent debts in the heart are sown,
Where rivalry blooms, though never shown.

Festivals gleam with a gilded light,
Anniversaries crowned in the gaudy sight;
As dreamers we walk in the shadow's keep,
Chasing rites that wound more than heal the weep.

Parents trade the care, for a care later returned,
Siblings share returnable gifts, their hands have earned;
Nations reflect it with their debts and pacts,
While life bends too low to its ancient acts.

Yet the bird feeds the chick with nothing to claim,
Fights the hawk's claw without any hope of fame;

And offers the sky's liberty to its fledglings' wings,
While man spills blood for the dust-bound things.

Where the Unseen asks for no coin nor trade,
Yet faith makes open deals many, in the shadow's shade;
And hearth, and school, and council gate,
Bear the same crest in the name of state.

All were meant, in the streams of truth,
To serve the whole, from age and youth;
Yet hands grow cold, and hearts forget,
When the minted gold becomes the net.

But when the tide of the play is known,
Selfish waves shall fall back from its throne;
For an eternal silence blooms Thy peace,
Where all vain bargains find its release.

Nature knows not the price tags of love,
It's coin perhaps the breath from near and the realms above;
And in that stillness, shadows cease,
Awakening truth, for eternal peace.

22

Falling in Love

Mind the unseen weaver of all threads,
Which looms through the time's unceasing treads;
Through forest deep and mountains high,
Beneath the earth, and above the sky—
Masking each life in a secret design,
Far from the truth's untraveled line.

Yet love is written even in the rains,
That falls to heal all withered veins;
From Heaven's vault it bends to kiss,
The roots and blades in a silent bliss;
Even in the drought's relentless breath,
Thy mercy descends, defying death.

The winds become the choral choir,
The rains the drums, the gales the lyre;
Notes that whisper, notes that roar,
Each a key to the hidden door;
A gift to the heart that leans to hear,
A truth the humble soul holds dear.

The wise may read the runes in streams,
The pure may hear Thee in their dreams;

The rivers may turn, the stars may stray,
Yet all are drawn in Thy hidden play;
And though the mind may miss the call,
The heart will follow, yielding all.

When night obscures the seeker's sight,
The moon unveils its milky, soothing light;
When the day inflames thy heart with fire,
A shade descends to cool thy desire.
Thou art the drink of the parched despair,
And thirst itself perhaps a holy snare.

No scripture holds Thy deepest reach,
Yet sun and streams speak the unknown reach;
No law shall bind, no threat shall move,
But a stillness wrapped in endless love;
No chaining nor stern commands,
Just the guiding of Thy gentle hands.

23

Scribbles

From a green-clad patch in gentle dales,
Where snow-topped hills lift the silver veils,
The evening sun spills its molten gold in flame,
On horizon's wide, and unending frame;
Till night, in robes of shadow deep,
Awakens from its patient sleep.

The clouds drift free as passing thought,
With anchor none, yet wonders wrought;
Their gilded rims in joys ignite,
Yet some cast spectres in the mind's dim light,
And myself, half awake, half in dream,
Still gazed upon the sky's mute theme.

These floating hosts in freedom roam,
Salute the sun in the crimson dome;
The firmament bows low in a grace,
While stars take up their shining place;
Each rune a silver, shifting unknown word,
A script the heart hast only heard.

As the drops unite in cloud's embrace,
To fall and kiss the earth's warm surface,

So are the soul born scribbles, rich and clear,
Break forth, when joy has brimmed the sphere;
And some will stand, their breath held tight,
To read Thy runes in the fading light.

Yet many pass with hurried eyes,
Still bound to earth, unheeding skies;
Chasing the green, the fleeting call,
They miss the cloud's true gift to all,
The whispered truth, in silence proud,
That drifts within a passing cloud.

24

The Window to Freedom

Besides the dancing sea, where the waves in chorus roar,
An alluring garden blooms on its shore,
Yachts daring the crests not far,
Ships shy away tracing cautious paths on deep, so far.

Spring hath poured its colours of marvel here,
Brushing leaves and blooms with shades in abundance,
A light winter breeze weaves through the scene,
This eve, in the deserted garth, hushed and waiting.

From the high nest atop a concrete tree, I gaze,
Closing the panes, turning to my luxuries within,
Music beats in the air, vibrant yet boxed,
After the day's labour, I sink to a cushioned rest.

Time's ticks push the evening along,
Dinner swallowed in a haste,
To the bed of comfort I retreat,
Dreaming not of stars, but of dawn's demands.

Yet the window stays shut,
The garden's call muted,
The breath of nature barred by curtains,
While the mind chases pleasing pleasures.

Still, all the time, the patient garden waits,
Its fragrance resting on the breeze,
Freshness poised to pour in,
If only, I unbolt my window, in a wish,
If only, I unbolt my soul, in a will,
That Thy eternal peace may flood me whole.

25

Invited Worries

Returning to roots, as a revenant to my village,
Met a few faces, yet hardly recall,
Who brought a scroll of sorrows and woes,
As though I were a mate from ancient days,
Inviting worry on their behalf, to share the pain in vain,
Or to cast an advice, proud in a gift of empathy,
Where I wonder: why worry for the illusive?

All strive to cross the ocean of this painful life,
Floating on its glittering surface in the shine of waves,
Yet in fret with tides, perilous and hideous,
Forget the strength of the depths beneath,
And choose to drift with the tide, cursing all the while,
And I wonder, why toil on the invited unreal?

Sacred scripts and chantings praise eternal love and care,
Hearts grateful in moments of grace, and proud in jubilation,
Yet in hours of comfort or woe, faith grows faint,
And the truth dims into the haze,
For the mind prefers the spice of agony over the nectar of delight,
As unseen manures, that tempt all away from the shine.

Rise or fall, joy or worry,
All the waves dissolve when sinking into the depths,
Where awareness accepts the tide's gifts in gratitude,
And dances with its rise and retreat.
Yet the cunning mind lures all towards the mirage,
And I wonder: why seek the false, forsaking the truth?

26

The Celestial Stage

Gazing anew at the sky so serene,
A gift of the dawn in silver sheen,
With more bright stars, than my mind could claim,
Or perhaps they bloomed in my dream's own frame.
Their twinkling whispers through silence glide,
Like waves of light on a cosmic tide;
They call to all with a voice so near,
Yet only, the patient one can truly hear.

Through the galaxy's arc they softly flow,
A milky mist in its tender glow,
Shaping a tunnel of brilliance wide,
Where Thy might gleams in majestic pride,
A garland vast on the night's dark gown,
Adorning the heavens as worlds drift down;
They dance in a rhythm no time can bind,
To a music unknown to the mortal mind.

They marvel on moves so swift, yet sure,
Each from its birth on a course secure;
All move in harmony's watchful grace,
No orbit astray from its fated place.
And I ask in an awe, what unseen hand,

Holds them steady; the sky, the sea, the land?
What anchors this grand and endless spin,
Where all spheres dance in the gravity's hymn.

O' whisper the secrets Thy cores conceal,
The rapture, no mortal can fully feel;
Speak of the freedom that knows no bars,
The boundless truth of the ancient stars.
Rocket my soul to Thy heights untold,
Through speeds no earthly eyes could behold;
Till I join that radiant, rushing stream,
To serve Thee well in a boundless dream.

27

The Stage on Land

At winter's door, the garden woke,
In blooms where light and fragrance spoke;
The night jasmine's pearls on shadows lay,
The Eugenia burned in bright arrays;
Till all air became a woven psalm,
A prayer of scent, both fierce and calm.

Then came the guests in winged delight,
With dragonflies in gold and night;
In ordered ranks, they swirled the air,
And they danced to the tunes of the secret prayer;
And butterflies came in painted streams,
Fulfilling the painter's quiet dreams.

From hidden realms their summons rose,
Through nectar's gates the dewdrop knows;
They hovered so close, yet heeded not,
The gaze of one who watched their plot;
Through dawn to dusk, in rites unbound,
They traced Thy patterns above the land.

Their fragile wings mocked human pride,
Where air parades in vain abide;

For borne by Thee, they never tire,
But feed on joy and holy fire;
They hold no past, they seek no more,
They dwell in 'Now', and Thee adore.

And I, still chained by thought's cold thread,
Asked why my soul takes flight instead;
Why not, like them, rise high and free,
To drink Thy grace in an eternal glow;
For both the stars and the blooms shall agree,
The stage is set, O' Lord, for me.

28

The Sparrow's Hymn

A pair of sparrows in a merry haste,
Gathered treasures with none to waste;
Threads and stalks, and bits of bark,
Wove their dwelling within leaves so dark.

I lingered still, with watching eyes,
Absorbing sparks of their enterprise;
Recalling my own restless quest,
For the shelter scarce in the city's chest.

Then came a storm with thundering cry,
That tore the calm of the midnight sky;
I feared their nest had met its doom,
And lay in sorrow through the gloom.

Yet the morning revealed their tireless art,
Undimmed in spirit, from a devoted heart;
With wings of trust, they built anew,
As though Thy hand had shaped them true.

Time rolled on, none noticed, yet on one bright dawn,
Tiny fledglings were gently drawn;
Perched with wonder, poised for their flight,
Guided in patience, bathed in light.

No worldly snare, no fleeting care,
Can bind the soul that learns to dare;
For even sparrows, frail and small,
Proclaim Thy play, sustaining all.

29

The Jewel of Life

Doubting the days that swiftly fly, all chase desires yet in vain,
Forsaking health for fleeting wealth, yet reaping only pain.
Not till the final gasp, we know the truth that waits so near,
That life's bright jewel was in hand, yet lost it in lust and fear.

All feign a busyness so grave, till death's dark pit they meet,
A weary race upon this earth, with hollow yet restless feet,
We preach against the tempting snares, yet wear their robes with unseen pride,
Spinning with lust's relentless wheel, until flung to death's cold tide.

Chained to the ticking hands of time, we play a shadowed part,
The stage applauds our passing role, but dust amass our own heart.

No beauty, fame, nor gold remains, when life's brief play is fully done,
For all we see, returns to silent earth, where all voices merge as one.

Some chase the shape of beauty's frame, in curves both soft or strong,
Yet all is but a fleeting scale, a short and shallow song that sung.
The body's grace, though praised today, will crumble into the bin of dust,
While only love and truth remain, eternal and pure, in a trust.

Awake, O' world, from slumber's mask, taste the freedom's living stream,
Ignite the flame of awareness bright, and drink from the life's holy dream.
Existence waits with patient love, unmeasured, for time unknown, undefiled,
Perhaps the purest gift of God to man — Thy mercy to his child.

30

Fires That Blind the Heart

All have tasted anger's flame,
Yet none could tell from whence it came;
We wear it proudly, as if a crown,
Yet in its fire, the brain burns down,
Blind to the truth, yet bound in shame.

From ego's seed, the fire is born,
A restless mind, a heart forlorn;
Anger and anguish, shadows twain,
Rise like a storm from a hidden plain,
Turning words to blades so sharp and keen.

Frustration bursts out unwittingly, when anger creeps unseen,
Taking us through vast plains of pain,
Forcing acts that seem in vain;
Yet knowing not, the response feeds anxiety,
While all follow the same in the sleepy society.

When Thou hast thrust thee to bud and bloom,
From chances millions, dispelling gloom,
For a blissful life, without any behests,

How can thee not trust Thy will and quests,
And left in intense spirits, to tackle life's own tests?

As Atman sparks both birth and death,
So the mind bestows or steals the breath;
Awake in grace, as it lights the skies,
But chained to pride, it blinds thy eyes,
And drags the soul to ruin beneath.

Anger speaks where weakness hides,
Where reason flees and love subsides;
It will not hear, it will not bend,
It has no truth, it makes no friend,
A fleeting storm on the restless tides.

Cage it not, nor strike it fast,
For bound, the spring will leap at last;
Instead watch with stillness, calm and true,
The false shall fade, the storm shall pass through,
And ego's mirage be overcast.

For saint and sinner, rich and poor,
All bow alike at the grave's dark door;
Crowns and masks are dust in time,
None may keep what is not thine,
Only the Real shall ever endure.

Anger, joy, and sorrow stray,
The clouds that veil the eternal way;
But life is a gift, a sacred breath,
A song that triumphs over death,
Perhaps in silent love, the truth holds its way.

31

Swindlers of Night

How can you rest in slumber deep,
When jagged dreams disturb your sleep?
Your webs are frail, your guile but small,
Awake! Taste truth, taste life to devour all.

You dream of darkness beyond any man's sight,
Or deep depths veiled in endless night;
Yet truth surrounds all the time, that you've never fled,
Nor slipped an inch from what God said.

Perhaps your terrors come as a grace,
To wake you up from that blind embrace;
Better fear that one which wakes the soul,
Than pride that swallows you as a whole.

You mask deceit in trust and care,
You bind the pure in secret snare;
But debts are tallied, fate is sure,
Your light will fade, your life obscure.

Yet still a path, though narrow, lies,
Before the breath within you dies;
Your coins, your praise, your worship's show
Cannot deceive the One who knows.

O' swindlers, turn, repent, and be clean,
Let heart and thought hold faith serene;
Restore and repay, while breath is thine,
And save thy seed by love divine.

Dedicated to a dear wolf in sheep's skin

32

The Natural Balance, Unseen

I sat in my hut at an eventide,
Watching the monsoon's silver ride,
The tiny garden drank the rain,
Its roots revived, its leaves made plain.

The greens bowed low in a grateful trance,
They swayed and turned in a sacred dance;
Twilight dimmed, and clouds took flight,
As droplets sang into the night.

They stirred up visions soft and deep,
That drifted through my mind, in sleep;
I woke up in haste to chase the skies,
Where dawn unveiled its fresh sunrise.

Yet aphids crept on leaf and stem,
Distracting me from bloom and gem;
I drove away the birds of the morn,
Unmindful of their hunger worn.

In days that passed, the insects grew,
The wary birds no longer flew;

The balance broke, my folly clear,
For nature's song was lost to my ear.

O' Lord, have mercy, light my way,
That I may see the truth each day;
To tend, not to mar, Thy garden's plan,
And walk in awe, as a true human.

33

The Maze of the Mind

All drift upon the tide of thought,
Yet few dare to seek the shore long sought.
The mind, perhaps twin-rivered in creation or ruin,
Spins shiny silver threads of bright illusion.
O' Lord, who keeps the silent Throne,
Unwrap this gift, all hearts have known.

We roam the maze of minds, our own hands have made,
Blaming the storm while the self seeds were laid.
Ego, the sentinel cloaked in unseen pride,
Builds smoky walls where shadows hide.
All eyes look outward, chasing skies,
Yet never wonder at the gaze it brings.

O' Keeper of the hidden key,
Teach us to rule, not to bend the knee,
On life's wide stage, where joy is crowned,
And all sorrows banished, cast to the ground,
The heart swells proud at the feast of praise,
But shrinks in pain when woe's chalice weighs.

From ego's coil spring word and deed,
That breaks the stillness where souls must feed,

O' Lord of the cosmos, no eye has seen,
Teach us to watch where the mind has been.
If denied its stream, the mind shall flood,
Carving a path through stone and mud.

What festers in darkness clings with might,
Till dawn dissolves it in the waves of light,
So lead us, O' Lord, to the mindful plain,
Beyond the fog of illusion's chain,
Let mind be the lantern, steady and free,
Not an ember lost to dust's decree.

For idle thought breeds fancies near,
Like desert winds make sand appear,
The restless heart still longs for Thee,
Though bound by chains it yearns to flee.
But the wondering soul, in stillness free,
Finds quiet songs that sing of Thee.

34

A Hymn at Dawn

Woke before the dawn, beneath the silent sky,
Here outside my hut where shadows lie;
The hush of stillness wrapped the air,
And the whispered truths beyond compare.

The full moon poured its milky grace,
A selfless glow, from a tender face;
Its soothing beams, like a stream so mild,
Embraced my soul, serene and wild.

Soft clouds drifted in play, veiling and apart,
Revealing the stars like jewels of art;
And Venus, the morning's radiant gem,
Bright from the east to crown the diadem.

The nightingale hushed her song at last,
While fleeting calls through darkness passed;
A flock took wing with dawn's delight,
Chirping their hymn to greet the light.

The trees stood still, like sages old,
The leaves bright with moonlight, washed in gold;
And the night jasmine, hidden yet profound,
Poured fragrant grace to fill the ground.

Enthralled, dissolved in the nature's breath,
I drank all the gifts, defying death;
Astonished, humbled, calm, and free,
In awe of all bestowed by Thee.

Hands raised, my gaze poised to heaven drawn,
A heart in brimming joy, mind's burden gone;
In a silent prayer, my soul took its wing,
To join the hymn, all beings sing.

35

The Snail

Human life, perchance, is as the snail,
Bound to a burden, yet destined to trail;
Dragging a shell that hinders the flight,
And feet that cling to the dust of the night.

Desire, the weight we polish and prize,
Chains of the mind that blind the eyes;
Chasing flavours that swiftly decay,
Trading our freedom for shadows of clay.

O' snail, a mirror to our passing span,
Ego the shell that encumbers man;
Built on illusions, fragile and vain,
It bends the soul to selfish gain.

Yet thou art patient in every strife,
Moving with a quiet acceptance of life;
While mortals, restless in borrowed creeds,
Are driven by greed to unholy speeds.

Perhaps Thy pace is slow, yet loyal and true,
Thy course unbroken by what blocks the view;
Neither exalting in the shine of joys,
Nor evading in sorrows that time employs.

Greasy sole may hinder thy way,
Yet still thou riseth to greet the day;
Silent pilgrim, meek, resigned,
A sermon writ for the restless mind.

Yes, snail of earth, thou teacheth me,
How burdens borne may yet set thy free;
How steady heart, through curbs unplanned,
May reach the truth by Thy guiding hand.

36

Awake Beyond the Dream

Dreams are familiar, gentle or dire,
From the shadows of memory, or sparks of desire;
The sleeper drifts, as a traveller blind,
Through deceiving visions of the mind.

In a silence deep the body rests,
Yet thoughts still weaves its endless quests;
Illusions shine, though false their gleam,
And life itself is but a dream.

For dreams though false can wound the heart,
Their unreal pains still leave a chart;
So too the mind with this cunning art,
Can tear the soul and keep it apart.

Accept not the lures that fade away,
Seek forth what no night could steal away;
Beyond the shady dens of want and strife,
There dwells the still, the eternal life.

O' Lord, remind us throughout our sleep,
A watch of Thine, patient, kind, and deep;
Call us again, till all may rise,
To be awake in truth, with opened eyes.

37

Two Ancient Trees

Two ancient trees in silence stand,
Planted by an immortal hand;
One holds life in its branches bright,
The other tempts with a borrowed light.

One bore the flame of the forbidden lure,
The other, breath of life evermore.
No tongue recalls when the play commenced,
Yet all pretend to know what happened.

As the tree of knowledge sharpens its taste,
Draws the other to an endless waste;
Where egos swell, and illusions rise,
And truth is veiled, and wisdom dies.

Through ages, men have claimed to know,
Yet sowed but war where peace should grow;
Their creeds like masks of the passing clay,
That bind their heart and leads it astray.

The fruit has fed both pride and pain,
Its harvest in loss, its wages in painful chain;
In dream and deed, man strays apart,
Forgetting love, forgetting the heart.

But still the tree of life hides not but abides,
In all, its root in secret silence hides;
Nurture it, that thy wings may touch the skies,
Forsake it, that every lure of ego dies.

The path is narrow, thorny and steep,
A few are awake, while many are asleep;
Yet those who walk with a patient breath,
Shall conquer fear, and trounce the death.

O' Lord, reveal Thy hidden flame,
Restore our souls, make us truly whole again;
That all good and evil shall fade away,
And peace eternal shall guide our ways.

For all the world is one great chord,
Played by Thy hand, O' silent Lord;
Where self, the witness, shines as the key,
And love alone is the road to liberty.

38

The Shine Behind the Veil

At times, impatience stirs my weary sleep,
To catch the pulses the dawn may keep.
As I rush outside with a heart so bright,
But now stood frozen beneath a starless night.

No moon, no cloud with silver gleam,
No winged song, no whispered dream.
Only a lamp from the street across, with its pallid glow,
A hushed world sleeping, dark and slow.

Perhaps the birds above still glide unseen,
The trees in trance, yet their fragrance leans,
The golden dawn I longed to find,
Is veiled by the slumber of my mind.

A sudden flash with the lightning's call,
Cool drops of grace begin to fall.
Soft bells echoed from a distant shrine,
Assuring prayers still rise to Thine.

The sun still burns, the moon still glows,
The stars still twinkle, the cloud still flows.
Yet shadows veil what always stays as truth,
As the mind blinds me in countless ways from the truth.

So I could raise thanks in dark or bright,
In storm or calm, in shade or light.
For every place is a shrine, when the veil is torn apart,
And then a tiny lightning strikes, a cognisance of my heart.

]

39

On Life's Fading Track

Days speed along on the world's worn track,
None who has gone shall ever come back,
Shadows grow long as the daylight wanes,
And time is a river that no hand can restrain.

Yet most missed the life, lost in its strife,
Chasing vain shadows that fractured their life,
While every heart keeps yearning for love,
For the grace that descends from the core above.

We tremble at endings, dreadful and untrue,
Blind to the light that is breaking through,
Shadows may threaten, despair may implore,
But destiny whispers: 'endure, and seek more'.

Born into the bonds, for the custom we bend,
Seeking a shine and peace, that is not the end,
Where glittering lures with its hidden hooks,
To distract our souls from the ancient books.

When trials defy man's law of life's way,
Forces the mind to forget the gifts of each day.
It curses the years and forgets the goal,
Blind to the worth of the deathless soul.

Days turn to dust, into a lifeless decay,
But the inner pulse still calls all to stay.
We must not let the play fade to grey,
Nor turn aside from Thy shining way.

40

The Choice-less Dawn

At the damp, serene hour of a dawn's first breath,
I stepped out of my lil hut to the earth's fresh breath.
The silver sky gleams, untouched, unchanged,
While the clouds drift dark, yet seem all pre-arranged.

A sudden scar of lightning cries-
"Nothing endures for ever but the Truth"
That lies beyond every play of joy and grief,
And beyond birth or death and the life in between.

Perhaps this secret is life's own art,
To live choice-less, away from the mind's own part,
To accept each gift, both grief and delight,
And allow space for gratitude before thy sight.
The rivers must flow on, though the banks may decay,
As the stars still return, though the night hides their way.
Seasons may falter as the wheel turns, yet the dawn shall rise,
Carrying whispers from Thy timeless skies.
The heart is a mirror, clouded with time,
When polished by silence, it learns to shine.
The pulse of the cosmos beats within all,
Which whispers gently, heed Thy eternal call.

For every moment of life is made anew,
With colours no spring will again imbue.
Each sorrow, each gladness stands alone,
Each passing instant, forever its own.

Rest, O' eyes, in the peace of release,
Wake to the shine of eternal peace.
The unseen energy draws all near,
Toward Thy light, where all is clear.

41

The Betrayal

"Renounce the world to seek peace," creeds proclaim,
Yet ego persists all the time, feeding its flame.
Man wars with nature for shadows unreal,
Wounding in masks Thy gem, too blind to heal.

Is it the world that betrays man's way?
Or is it the man who betrays the sacred play?
In joy we feast on gifts so bright,
But in greed, we call the world a blight.

We stray from nature, in dream's disguise,
Chasing desires with blinded eyes,
We bow to ego, false and in vain,
Bound in delusion, to be bound in pain.

The mind enslaves all with cunning art,
Blaming the world to shield its part,
Yet dawn still whispers, soft and true:
Awake, discern the false from the true.

A tiny stream of truth still flows within,
Unclouded by the desires or by thy sins.
Its waters will cleanse the stains of strife,
And call all back to the only source of life.

Forsake the glitters, the passing show,
The seeds of sorrow that ego sows,
Return my soul to the primal song,
Where silence silently declares, all belonged all along.

42

Seeking Thee

If I were a flower, shaded, yet small,
I'd pour my fragrance and give my all,
Till my petals fell with no return,
But a silent gift for hearts that yearn.

If I were a stream with branching hands,
I'd quench the thirst of many barren lands,
Flowing to the palms, both faint and near,
Bringing calmness to minds sincere.

If I were a spring, 'twixt heat and frost,
I'd scatter colours the world has lost,
And fill the air with a fragrant song,
Proclaiming Thee, to whom all belong.

If I were the soil beneath each root,
I'd wait in patience, calm and mute,
Nourishing all seeds in Thy vast play,
As Thou dost wait for my return one day.

If I were a cloud in the boundless sky,
I'd wear Thy wisdom as I fly,
Till thinned to nothing, to disappear,
Yet leave Thy sparks for all to consider.

If I were a mountain, tall and still,
I' d stand as a witness to Thy will,
Bearing the storms, the sun, and the rain,
Yet bowing low in Thy domain.

If I were the fire with a leaping flame,
I' d burn away both pride and fame,
Consuming myself till none remains,
But only Thee in endless reigns.

If I were a singer with mortal breath,
I' d hymn Thy love through life and death,
And vanish into the song once more,
As a note returning to the Core.

If I were a player of strings and keys,
I' d spare my hands in melodies,
Pouring each note in a gratitude,
Upon Thy stage with an unseen fortitude.

If I were a scripter of the silence deep,
From wordless wells Thy truth I' d reap,
Inscribing the bliss till my arms give way,
Yet telling, still of Thy brightest ray.

If I were a star in the midnight dome,
I' d shine Thy light and guide souls home,
And when the fire at last grew dim,
I' d fall again to rest in Him.

If I were a dream at the edge of sleep,
I' d cradle Thy secrets soft and deep,

And when the dawn dissolves the night,
I'd wake again in Thy pure light.

If I could walk through time's vast dome,
I'd search all the stars to find Thy home,
Through the loneliest corners my steps would trace,
Still seeking signs of Thy hidden tread or face.

If I were darkness, void and cold,
I'd find the courage to be bold,
Dissolving into Thy radiant glow,
As a particle lit with love to show.

If I were a droplet in the cloud's height,
I'd rise in joy, then fall in a fate of flight,
Returning deep into Thy boundless sea,
Forever lost, yet to be found in Thee.

If I were a ray with swiftness bright,
I'd race in haste to Thy shrine of light,
Dissolve at last in Thy embrace,
And bloom once more in Thy soft grace.

For flower or stream, light or flame,
All Thy forms return to Thee the same;
Each birth, each death, a holy strand,
Forever held in Thy vast hand.

And when at last all roles are done,
The play dissolves for all, yet Thou art One.

43

Thy Throne and Thy Footprints

Where mighty stars bow low in grace, to tunes of an endless chime,
Where the nebulae in a swirling dance to keep perfect, gentle on time,
Where comets wild, in fiery flight, now halt and humbly bend,
Where rainbows weave their secret arcs in marvels without an end,
Where light-years hide from time's domain, to taste Thy eternal truth,
There lies Thy throne, and Thy footprints bright, in an ageless, deathless youth.

Where light, both seen and unseen, streams to one embracing space,
Where darkness claims no birth nor end, no measure and no place,
Where joy and sorrow fade away, and peace and love abide,

Where pain and laughter, both alike, to the holiness that confides,
Where none but Thee in presence reigns, free from all the earthly rules,
There lies Thy throne, Thy footprints pure, where love alone still rules.

Where secret songs on unknown waves enchant the listening ear,
Where hidden gems of eternal craft shine though no eyes draw near,
Where the fragrant emptiness dissolves the chains of thought and mortal will,
Where sacred love bestows its grace unseen in harmonies so still,
Where holy silence glows with light any mortal eye can not see,
There lies Thy throne, Thy footprints true, in Thy boundless mystery.

Where the rivers of creation rise or fall into a silent flow,
Where the seeds of spheres are born unknown, the mortal cannot know,
Where breath of the angels fans the flame of stars that will never fade,
Where the heaven's loom in secret hands its golden threads has laid,
Where every soul, once lost in the darkness, awakens clear and whole,

Where dust becomes a crown of fire, illumined as same as the soul,
There shines Thy throne, O' Lord of all, beyond both time and space.

O' Lord, ascend or draw us towards the realms no soul has known,
Where words fall silent, acts grow still, and only Thy truth is shown,
Where mind and thought, in a humble awe, their nothingness confess,
And melt into the secret and sacred void of Thy divine caress,
There, let this tiny drop of dust in Thy vast ocean be,
To dwell forever in peace, in love's eternity.

44

A Friendly Quarrel

From the green backyard came cries so clear,
Treepies clashed as babblers drew near.
Through the window I bent to gaze,
And stepped outside in quiet amaze,
Yet they all, absorbed in a feathered fray,
Took no heed of my watchful eyes that day.

Perhaps it was a nest they'd defend,
Or a stolen morsel they'd amend;
But not of gold, not of land, not any human greed,
But only nature's passing need.
No blood was spilt, no lasting pain,
The quarrel passed like a gentle rain.

And I, a witness to their play,
Began to muse in my own way:
Why does my race, with laws so strict,
Still seek to harm, to wound, and inflict?
We march in force on land and wave,
And fill the world with ash and grave.

For causes of shadows born in vain,
We sow destruction, death, and pain,

If we could sense from nature's call,
To guard, to clash, yet never to maul,
Then earth would turn in a gentle peace,
And wars of pride at last would cease.

45

The Cages Unknown

Perhaps we all are subtly bound,
By selfish dreams where truth is drowned,
A cunning cage the mind hast spun,
That blinds us 'til our days are done.
We chase the shimmering desert's light,
Yet turn from truth, though in our sight.

Perhaps we face the hardest unreal cell,
Our own mind's prison wrought so well;
And knowing not, all walk in a sleep,
Through gilded walls that still run deep,
In wealth and power's fleeting flame,
Pretending freedom in a luring game.

Perhaps our minds have tied the veil,
That keeps our finest vision frail;
And though a lightning bliss may break,
Its flash too brief for hearts to wake,
While all choose the cage, the lie, the known,
And turn from the truth's eternal throne.

Perhaps the mind, in a shadowed beast,
Resists the dawn, and denies the best;

With potions dark and poisons near,
It feeds the mask, sustains thy fear,
For ego's false, unyielding pride,
Which conceals the wisdom buried deep inside.

Perhaps, O' Lord, in unawareness,
We waste our lives in gilded snares;
Yet still Thy love and mercy sows its seed,
And calls all from our endless greed,
Awake, arise, from the slumber flee,
That the best may bloom internally and eternally.

46

Ruined Temples

In humble shrines of earthen clay,
Thou dwellest still in a bright array;
Yet blind, we break the temple's frame,
To feed the dream to ego's claim,
Once pure and free, the mind began,
Till craving grew through ways of man.

Few seek the roots where life took its start,
Or trace the map of thy soul's own chart;
All strive to cross the sea of tears,
Chasing the mirage of their tamed years.
Yet still the soul, in a patient tone,
Calls us back to what is prior known.

O' hear the whispers from the deep,
Where truth's eternal treasures buried deep;
The spring of power, pure and wise,
Awaits the heart that learns to rise.
Unveil the inner, make it sharp and clear,
To catch the call, as the truth draws near.

Awake, and fling wide the heart's own door,
To find the shrine and shine forevermore;

Where none may enter, as saved as a seen birth,
Or cross the veil when leaving the earth.
Rebuild Thy temple, pure and true,
And merge, to Thee whom all are due.

47

A Tree's Soliloquise

Still recall the blessed power,
That burst me from my sheltered bower;
Like a sprout from seed, to stem I grew,
Thy air my guide, Thy light my view;
Nature's bounty freely fed my frame,
And all the time I was a witness in gratitude,
To rise, and to reach the heights designed,
In tune with the play, in my heart, as destined.

The rains ran short, the storms would rage,
Yet Thou would shield in every stage;
Through drought and flood, through the trial's sting,
I learned to bloom every spring;
I asked not who my fruits would feed,
Nor where my scattered seeds might lead,
I swayed in joy through sun and shade,
And danced to the music, the existence hast made.

I knew not time had drawn its line,
Till an axe struck deep through the spine of mine;
I guessed not why, nor sought to know,
What humans reap, or why they sow;
I met the end in steady peace,

In silent prayer, in calm's release;
No pain could touch, no grief could bind,
While still the truth held all my hand.

Now at Thy feet my thanks I lay,
Before my form returns to clay;
The part is done, my stage is bare,
Yet still the play moves everywhere;
O' Light, touch the human hearts anew,
That they may plant as a few more new,
So life may bloom eternally,
And keep the play till infinity.

48

Life - A Sacred Game

Life may be but a sacred game,
Between birth and death, as we name;
A dance of chances, bright and rare,
To play with joy, to breathe the air,
Through countless forms, in garbs unknown,
To seek the place we call our own;
Till as an empty soul within our heart,
The home long whispered by the heart.

Yet oft deceived, not by the way
That all have walked in mortal clay,
But by the lures of the tempting prize,
That blinds the heart and veils the eyes;
When turning back, when I sought the ways,
A thousand walls confronted in many ways;
And at the end, my ledger read to me,
More failings marked than the years I'd tread.

I thought, perhaps, the rogue may fare,
No worse than those who choose the fair;
For who on earth can weigh the right,
Or bring Thy justice into thy sight?
The scales of good and ill we keep,

May not be Thine, so high, and so deep;
For perhaps the truth and love aid the measure,
To keep the balance fair and true, yet unknown.

Though clothed in silks, we yet are bare,
If pride and greed are all we wear;
The masks we prize as worldly gold,
May hide a heart both dim and cold;
Thy marks for triumph none can see,
Nor guess the weights that crown the free;
For all that glitters in our dreams,
May vanish in Thy truer beam.

Still starving for that long- lost shore,
From misdeeds of past and false allure,
I crave the feast I' ve never known,
The truthful light before Thy throne;
Lo' illusions, no longer tempt or bind,
With ego' s chains and mists of mind;
But let the veil be torn away,
That truth may shine in boundless ways.

49

The Odyssey

All know the salmon's silvered grace,
A feast to heal and health embrace;
Its flesh a gift to the flesh of man,
To lengthen life as nature can,
A form so near to perfect made,
In service to the world displayed.

Yet few discern the tale they bear,
Through ocean's vast unbounded air;
Till grown to fullness, called to play,
They turn from the salt's unending sway,
And seek the narrow, winding stream,
To find the spring from which they came.

Against the tide, they press and leap,
Through rapids fierce and currents deep;
They climb the falls where few could stand,
And flee the hungry jaws of every land;
Though wearied, wounded, pressed with strife,
They guard the thread that binds their life.

No thought for pain, no voice to blame,
They reach the place from which they came;

To lay their young on chosen ground,
Where safety, love, and care abound;
And then, in gift so pure, they give,
Themselves that their own kin might live.

What holy fire their hearts must keep,
To spend their years, and sow so deep;
Through death's sure gate, with joy to go,
Fulfilling what Thou didst bestow-
A crown of purpose, bright and high,
To end the race in joy and never sigh.

Yet humankind, so proud in name,
Complaints in plenty, shuns the flame;
With restless want and hearts untrue,
They miss the laws the salmon know.
O' Lord, teach us that steadfast way,
To live, to give, and to end the role,
So when death's shadow claims the shore,
We join the Ocean forevermore.

50

Untie All Chains From Shore

Untie the chains that bind this boat,
From worldly shore where anchors float;
And set the prow to radiant seas,
Where truth's deep currents move with ease.
Let love and peace be the wind and oar,
To break the beliefs that chained all before.

For trust and belief are not the same,
Though oft they wear a kindred name;
Belief may bind us near the sand,
To join the crowd on the solid land.
We row, yet never drift away,
Still moored where we began the day;
A ship on shore may seem secure,
But that is not what ships are for.

Like caged but winged birds, we long to rise,
To taste the breadth of the boundless skies;
No threat could steal our living breath,
Saving the chains that cause the wing's slow death;
We live as captives in a prison, yet unaware,

While life's great wheel turns through the air;
O' leave the shore, for the dream not untrue,
And find the real so near to thee.

To trust is to drink from the stream we can taste,
To believe is to wander where shadows are placed.
The sun stands crowned in the court of the skies,
The moon sails silver where the still night lies;
The stars keep watch in their jewelled array,
Trust walks the path where light holds the way,
Belief treads softly where veils still stay.

For trust and faith may walk apart,
Although joined within the seeker's heart;
Belief is shaped from birth's first day,
Yet trust will sail the seeker's way;
Beyond the bounds, beyond the bars,
Through rippling waves and guiding stars;
Where truthful hand will guard the way,
Past all joys and griefs, to an endless day.

51

Visit to an Edifice

I marched in step with throng and crowd,
Like a slave to drum and prayer were made aloud;
I reached the place all deemed so high,
Beneath its roof, yet beneath the sky.
Oft had I come in days before,
Yet now a strangeness touched my core.

The chants rose, and the hymns were strong,
As if the air itself was a drifting song;
The multitude, with their outstretched hands,
Besought Lord's will for promised lands,
With gifts of coins, of candle's flame,
To turn aside both grief and shame;
To bargain joy for sorrow's due,
As though Thy love were bought anew.

I stood apart, yet in their ring,
A stranger to the preying prayers in offering;
The air was thick with hope's demand,
And prayers for fate to change its hand.
And I wondered alone, has not this sacred place,
Been dimmed by selfish, pleading grace?

For long ago, one soul did prove
That holiness is truthful, selfless love.

I could not speak as they did speak,
Nor join the cries the weary seek;
Perhaps the world would mark me all wrong
For the silence in the temple throng,
Yet in my heart I knew the way,
To bow in thanks with Thy own play.
O' guide my steps through ways unseen,
To Thy pure realm where truth is clean.

52

Fragmented Mind

All humans strive in ceaseless fights,
For gold, for name, for vaunted heights;
Upon a scrap of muddy ground,
Where the migrants' footsteps slip around;
The endless march, the fraying tread,
Leaves lives worn thin, yet unnoticed,
Where the deep within, still fresh, untamed,
A breath unclaimed, unnamed, still remains.

A thousand masks in our secret keep,
In mind's dark closet, buried deep;
To suit each hour, each crowd, each role,
They hide the wounds that haunt the soul;
Yet all the while, the lantern waits,
To shine through self's deceiving gates,
And light the void, that space so wide,
Where wisdom blooms and truth abides.

For pride and piety, meek and mild,
Each mask is woven, each mood beguiled;
In market's loudness or in temple's still,
The shifting face obeys thy will.
And all the while, the master mind,

Commands a change for every kind;
Its wardrobe vast, its hunger wide,
Yet never meets the self inside.

These masks, in turn, do bind the flesh,
To phantom thoughts in colours fresh;
They play their part, they change, they fade,
Till life's clear stream is overlaid.
But in the quiet's tender core,
A whisper calls, from a distant shore,
Where mind is whole and masks are none,
And sails are loosed to meet the truth.

O Lord, lead forth from shore to sea,
Where empty mind and truth agree;
Unmoor our hearts, undo the ties,
And guide us home through boundless skies.

53

Simplicity

Through the mists I row, past the ghostly shore,
Where masked faces drift, as lanterns hollow to the core;
Each feigns meekness, humble guise they spread,
Yet move in the dark like the walking dead;
Eyes shut fast to the sunrise of light,
Blind to the dawn that dissolves the night.

They barter in circles of weary design,
Drinking from wells where false loves shine;
In dreamscapes woven of fragile illusion,
They whisper of virtue yet live in confusion;
For beneath their cloaks, the riddle is clear,
Being simple is not so simple here.

This carnival plays with mien's own' thread,
White cotton torn robes crown the "pure" instead.
Vegan hands raise the chalice of earth,
While the poor in their rags are denied their worth,
The rich wear masks of a saintly face,
While truth runs buried, denied its place.

For here where painted virtues parade in play,
And graces are trained and polished to display,

The river of honesty flows far and deep,
Beyond all appearances that men may keep;
The hidden refrain the wise hearts recall:
Being simple is not that simple at all.

54

Lonely Star

Beneath Thy boundless midnight dome, I watched the silent play unfold,
Where the highs wore a cloak of gloom, with neither star nor twinkle bold,
A few thin silver wraiths of cloud, like wanderers lost in realms up there,
Drifted apart, to fade away in darker hands that claimed them there.

Yet a diamond, lone and bright, pressed forth through the shadows deep,
It pierced the night in fearless gleam, refusing clouds's claim to keep.
Probably it came to mark my path, my faltering steps, my trials' climb,
To whisper soft, with a secret smile, Thy guard hast stayed through every time.

The moon, too, wrestled in the shrouds, with patient strength, in silver might,
Straining to break the sable chains that dimmed the deserving light.
In an entreat or by a command, and I could not decode

the moon's decree,
As the moon strove to free the star, and let its gentle shining spread in grace.

Though clouds may strive and tempests roar, their light breaks forth for sure,
Straining to break the sable chains that dimmed the deserving light.
So let no storm, nor shadow's weight, obscure their glow, nor veil their grace,
For in their watch my soul recalls, a cosmos brimming with Thy care.

55

The Incredible Craftsman

Upon a withered palm I gazed, a winged craftsman there I found,
Clothed in robes of brown and white, with a crown of fire on its head,
Thy brush had painted its feathered frame with colours from the sun,
And set it to its playful yet patient task, till Thy sacred work was done.

With a tapping beak, like a sage in quest, it tested the bark with care,
Etching a circle flawless and bright, as drawn by a compass rare;
The geometry not trained by men, nor born of human pride,
But whispered deep within the heart, where all Thy laws abide.

For days it carved, then vanished into the wind's soft hymn,
And returning weeks thereafter, as if to bless the rim;
"O' little master," I wondered then, "what dwelling calls thee home?

Who sends thee forth on tasks alike, though trackless skies remain to roam?"

No wages claimed, no hoarded gain, no ledger kept in hand,
Yet freely did it labour on, as Thou didst thy command;
While humans cry out, in lack of time for tenderness and love,
This winged one gave all its time, with strength from Thee above.

And soon the gift stood waiting there, a chamber pure and complete,
Till parrots dressed in emerald green made it their chosen seat;
The craftsman gone, its task fulfilled, no boasts upon the air,
No shadow stained the holy work, no pride was hidden there.

O' bird of breath, a disciple true, the divine creed I long to know,
To give without a thought of self, to reap no debt on task below;
To move in step with secret clocks that only heaven knows what it keeps,
To trust that love that provides the bread, while every human creeps in sleep.

Teach me, thy voice of feathered hymn, the law by which you live,

That I may carve within my heart, not the ego but the joy of how to share;
And when my days like sand are spent, and the life's last tide has flown,
May I, like thee, leave gifts behind that others call their own.

56

Engrossed By the Wonders of Nature

When half the year had softly flown, the monsoon took its hurried leave,
Dark clouds withdrew their silver sighs, no more their soothing tears to weave;
And the sky, now crystal clear, revealed the starry realm above,
A midnight sea of jewelled gems, in silent chains of wonder's love.

I gazed upon that endless spread, recalling dreams from my younger days,
The stalwart stars that kept their post, in ancient, unrelenting blaze;
How strange to think they still abide, while mortal flesh must soon fade away,
Yet bid me drift amongst their dance, where silent songs of heaven play.

Some shone so near with burning pride, some far as whispers can't reach,

Yet all beguiled my yearning soul, with truths no human tongue could teach;
A comet passed as a wandering guest on stage, in playful arcs its trail it cast,
And bowed in jest to all it met, before it slipped into the darkness past.

Below, the tiny fireflies dared compete, with tender glows that softly gleamed,
They lit the tree with earthly stars, like sparks from fancies the forest dreamed;
They vanished then to rest in leaves, content to guard the shadowed deep,
While higher vault kept the watch above, in solemn silence vast and steep.

O' Lord, I bow in a humbled awe, at marvels vast and wonders near,
The fiery worlds beyond my grasp, the fleeting lights I hold so dear;
For man so often forgets the bliss, in futile chases, blind and far,
Yet life is here, in fireflies close, and in the whispers of stars so far.

57

The Darkness

Lo', all eyes that gazed upon the weary earth,
Ye saw its treachery masked in mirth:
Lo' all ears that lingered in the hush of night,
Ye caught the whispers that eluded the light:
So long have souls in dreaming gloom been bound,
Bartering truth for coins that turn unsound:
Till darkness, grown familiar to their sight,
Reveals the secret buried in its night in light.

The scrolls of old still scream of light and flame,
Yet man pursues but shadows of the same in shame:
Around the heart they wander, blind and unwise,
Yet never touch the fire that never dies;
They wrestle darkness as a foe to kill,
Striking in vain with blind and restless will;
Unknowing still that the shadow yields away,
Not by the hand, but by the birth of a day.

For none by sword can chase the night apart,
Nor silence flee by clamour of the heart;
It bows, it melts, it trembles into flight,
Before the first dawn's ray of holy Knight;

That beam reveals the wellspring pure and true,
And paints the world in the morning's blissful hue,
Till the land once shrouded, broken, cold, and grim,
Resounds in joy and bathes in the light with the Knight.

The night shall fade as a dew before the sun,
Its shadows scattered, having nowhere to run.
The veil unravelled falls in a threadbare grace,
And truth shines clear upon the creation's face.
The heart, long captive, finds its chains undone,
Its pulse united with the eternal One.
No more in dream-born terrors shall it bend,
For the dawn with Thee, is dawn without an end.

58

Blind to the Quiet Truth

Dawns and dusks in quiet grace crown each newborn day,
Each one a fresh painting, brushed in light's array;
Nature sways in its rhythm, soft but sure in flow,
Trusting the endless dance of the sun's rise and glow;
Where the winged choirs soar with songs that kiss the sky,
While others rest in stillness, letting moments drift by;
All the life, feathered, furred, or rooted in the ground,
Offer gratitude in silence, each a holy hymn to Thee .

Mankind walks past this blessed stage in hurry, unaware,
Past morning's cooling breath, past twilight's tender air;
Not in longing humble, but in rivalled faiths of creeds,
Perhaps blind to the quiet truth all souls most need;
Still, these moments wait, with fragrance rich and deep,
For any heart that pauses, for any soul to keep;
Yet most men see not the radiance close at hand,
Nor the greater glow where lanterns of the spirit stand.

The faiths and woven prayers are rivers to the one and only sea,
Each belief a vessel to carry each heart, a pilgrim free;

Though the world holds many tongues, in truth, there is no fight,
For Thou shalt hear every whisper in equal, in holy light;
Why burden nature with the relentless chants in haste,
Whilst Thy own calm wonders around, are never laid to waste;
Watch how the river moves, unhurried yet complete,
Watch how the steadfast trees so high, greet each dawn it meet.

Let us keep up the play like rivers - grateful, calm, and clear,
Let our hearts unbound by hurry, our minds unshaped by fear;
Let kindness be our compass, and mercy be our way,
Let patience be the lantern that lights each fleeting day;
Breathe in deep, the gifts of morning, and bless each twilight's hue,
For every shade of beauty holds a trace of Thou;
Attuned to the creation's hum, yet steady as a stone,
And rest in the knowing: 'Thou art here with me'.

59

The Radiant River

Oft have I pondered where all sins are born,
And where their crooked roots take hold, forlorn,
Against the rhymes of the heaven's tune,
As men walk narrow lines beneath the sun.
They call some virtues, to chase rewards unseen,
Are like shadows lost in Thy eternal sheen.

Deeds, though cloaked in rectitude, are vain,
If conscience sleeps, or bows to gain.
Not from the well where truth resides,
But from the halls where ego hides.
Pilgrims return with alms in hand,
Yet seek men's praise, not Thy command.
As though heaven's wealth were trinkets of coin,
While treasures eternal await hearts that join.

A cup brimming with milk spills only white,
And one filled with love pours out peaceful light,
Perfuming all with fragrance born of grace;
But cups of dust afloat in milk's embrace,
Gathers nothing but the dust it bears,
Blind to the gift that floats unaware.

To turn a deaf ear to the whisper within-
Is this not the root from which all sins begin?
For the mind, enslaved to flashing desire,
Strangles the truth with its fading smoke;
Yet when the mud is filled with Thy rays,
All sins dissolve in the dawn of the blaze;
And what then flows from the humbled heart,
Is the sea of trust Thou dost impart.

60

A Festivity Eternal

In a world starving for festivity, where wonder's thread is torn,
All chase illusions, blind to the light that greets each dawn,
Where costly firecrackers rival the aura of northern lights in vain,
While humble hearts sit silent, missing the truth's bright reign.

They seek far lights they cannot name,
Weaving joys from desire's fleeting flame.
Yet the true feast, in radiance pure and free,
Awaits unseen in eternity's endless sea.

Many stain life's chalice with pride and claim,
To lock themselves in quarrels, calling it peace by name.
Assassinate in the name of love or peace, yet pretend blind,
Always missing the freedom only truth can find.

Eyes fixed on petals, striving for grander hue,
Forgetting the thread that binds all, to the sacred view.

Hidden beauty blooms where the greed cannot tread,
Into the feast eternal, where love is fed and spread.

O' hearts that wander in the shadowed race,
Rest awhile in Thy embracing grace,
Let the mind grow still, the soul receive the grace,
In a radiant feast, in which all the rest entrust.
Let not the clamour of classes mislead,
Nor flashing joys their falsehoods breed.
For in the silence, the true song rings,
And the soul drinks the freedom it brings.

61

The Silent Sentinel

Max, my Lab, with curious eyes that gleam,
Walks with me through a waking dream;
His innocence grants my heart its celestial wings,
And lifts me past the earth's fading things.

When I tease with shadows sharp and near,
He greets them all with trust, not rage nor fear,
A gaze where hidden heavens dwell unseen,
And in that silent smile, all my darkness lean.

To strangers' step, his growl a growing flame,
A sentinel none could dare to tame;
Yet by my side, his spirit glows so smooth,
Softer than the dawn's first silvered snow.

While man's mortal kin, in pride's disguise,
Raise the ego's sword to guard their side,
Where Max stands unarmed, steadfast and pure,
A love that no wound could e'er obscure.

Perhaps all humans mirror this same plight,
Fearing God in all they claim or cite;
Lacking trust in a love unseen,
Yet chanting prayers in a reverent sheen.

For others run through veils unbroken,
Chasing crowns from fears unspoken;
But Max still waits where love runs deep,
Perhaps a vow the timeless angels keep.

While men may hide in fear's disguise,
Max greets the truth with loyal eyes;
No creed, no mask, no false defence,
Just simple, boundless innocence.

And when my path grows dim and far,
He leads me past each dying star,
To fields no earthly map hast shown,
Where weary souls at last find their home.

62

The Darkest Art of Bondage

The darkest yet worst art of bondage part,
Is when the captive loves their part;
When the shiny iron chains seem soft to wear,
And lull the soul to slumber there.

Y'all are not the flesh that fades to clay,
Nor the restless mind that drifts away;
But a seed from realms where the stars are sown,
An unseen spark of the Infinite's own.

Quail not the Gods that men have made,
Nor the devils wrapped in mortal shade;
For both shall pass like the morning mist,
Their reign a dream that can't persist.

Instead, in a reverent silence bow,
To the formless truth that holds thee now;
The Might unseen beyond the cosmos, yet ever near,
Whose voice is truth and whose light is care.

Awake, O' soul, from shadows deep,
Rise from the chains that bid you sleep;

The empyrean waits with the gates flung wide,
A boundless sea of freedom, a radiant tide.

Drink not from cups of fleeting night,
But taste the wine of deathless light;
For ye were born of timeless flame,
An eternal child, in Thy true name.

63

Ashes of the Banners

The soldier walks where shadows bleed,
For colours stitched in a mortal greed of creed;
He strikes his brother, with a heart so frozen,
For tiny clothes that claim the earth their own.

In midnight dreams, a whisper calls,
Through smoky veils, through crumbling walls;
Yet far away, his heart would flee,
To hearths now lost beyond the sea.

The stars above in a balance stay,
Their unseen course will never decay;
But man, unbridled, breaks the scale,
And drives himself through storm and hail.

He builds his thrones on dust and bone,
Yet dies as bare as he was born;
The banners fade, the trumpets cease,
What endures is neither thy love nor peace.

When warplanes go mute and swords grow still,
When silence bends all the battle's will,
In the end, there lies no crown, no victor's prize,
Just ashes drifting through the skies.

64

Assuring Night Skies

Fortunate am I to stand beneath December's skies,
Where seasons hides its face in strange disguise;
Damp and heavy, it withholds the promised breeze,
Yet dawn unfolds with whispers soft, above the tender seas.

The sky, a patient sage, composes drifting signs,
In silver threads and shifting mystic lines;
But hurried souls, with eyes on flashy gain,
Perceive not the script through veils of rain.

I, frail in frame yet starved in soul's desire,
Reach for the hidden words, the script of fire;
There clouds of silver and dark, proud in stately flight,
Quarrel playfully with the kin of brooding night.

Beyond their clash, the jewelled watchmen stay,
The silent stars that never lose their way;
They call me inward, and Thy tongue is clear,
A language loud within, yet none may hear.

For truth shines not in thunder's might or flame,
But in the lantern's glow, too soft to name;

And I, a speck adrift on the eternal tide,
Behold the Boundless, mirrored deep inside.

O' eternal prompts, scripted high above,
What glitters in the skies is but the love,
That waits to waken in each human heart,
Is the Abode of light, of which we are a tiny part.

65

The Unseen Seed of Eternity

I cradled seeds within my hand,
For the messengers of sky and land;
How frail their coats, yet the power deep inside,
The sun itself and all the stars abide.

They wait in a silence, hushed and still,
Yet dream of heights, of light, of will;
And I, perhaps, am such a core,
Unopened yet, yet holding more.

Around me, masks of men parade,
In borrowed robes their hands have made;
While the seeds wear garments plain and true,
That hide no lies, to birth the truth.

The spark eternal dwells in all,
Yet few will hear its hidden call;
They trample kin in a frenzied race,
And lose the bloom of thy inner grace.

We chase the smoke, the easy prize,
And bind ourselves with gilded ties;

While deeper still, the soil conceals,
The truth that waiting, the silence that heals.

O' Men far better to bow, to rest,
To fold the restless wings of quest;
Till roots awake and the upward climb,
To blossom in the light sublime.

66

Unity A Might

Upon a mango bough at rest,
The magpie-robin built its nest;
With some bulbuls near, in the leaf and shade,
No quarrel still, for their kingdom made.

No painted plume, though rich and rare,
Yet could match the life that sparkled there;
A chest so small, yet a song so strong,
Where the seeds and insects turned to dawn.

The hummingbird, a jewelled flame,
At the flowers whispered the same:
"You too are small, yet life ye bear,
The wonder flows through all who share."

The breeze became the preacher's voice,
The golden rays, the hymn of choice;
Each leaf and blade, each trunk and the sun,
In silence joined, yet rose as one.

But in the man's way, clans and banners stand,
With broken oaths and grasping hands;
He calls it peace, yet builds for war,
And scars the soil with blood once more.

Yet nature's choir in truth replies:
"Unity lifts the souls to skies;
But where false accords in greed began,
Shall wither, though they boast they've won."

67

Thy Book of Life

There lies an open book, beneath the boundless skies,
As humble as the morning dew, yet vast where wonder lies;
Not writ with ink, nor bound by mortal hands,
But traced in the breath of living flame, right across the sea and land.

Yet man, grown weary of the pages of his soul,

Seeks the tongues of interpreters to mend and to make him whole;

He quails when winds of trial arise, and in trembling turns away,
Petitioning for comfort's balm, while truth stands as plain as a day.

Look rather to the river's course, and the patient, rooted tree,
The bird whose hymn is born of joy, not any flattery's decree;
They crave no counterfeit of praise, nor hollow human fame,
They walk the eternal script, and glorify Thy name.

But man, in sermons robed with pomp, in rites that veil his eyes,
Has bound himself with cords of pride and darkened the living skies;
The text of life he will not read, though written clear and near,
For louder sounds his masked tale, than Thy soft voice to hear.

Each breath, each shifting cloud above, each rustling of the leaf,
Holds stories whole and infinite, but complete beyond thy belief;
Yet blinded by his restless dreams, man fashions worlds his own,
And misses what Thou dost inscribe on air, on fire and on stone.

Awake, O' soul, before Thou shall turn the page away,
The present is a jewel bright, much radiant than thy day;
Read deeply in the dawn's ascent, and in branches bends with the breeze,
The silence hidden within the notes of birds and of singing trees.

Truth dwells not in tombs of the past, nor in tomorrow's shade,
It lives within the 'Now' alone, where all is seen and made;
But man still wanders in memory's waste, and fears of days to come,

While all his years like dunes dissolve, timeless truth stands alone.

Only in stillness of the heart, awareness finds the way,
Only in the light of Now, Thy Kingdom shines as a day;
As a seal is set on every breath, Thy signature so divine,
A language not of mortal tongue, but soul in trust may sign the note.

68

Rays of Truth

I stumbled on a tale of old,
Where light's true essence once was told,
To one whose eyes had never seen,
Yet claimed to know what light must mean.

A blind monk stood in bold debate,
Declaring all were false, though indeed great;
The listeners knew, yet bowed in grief,
For none could pierce his dark belief.

Creeds rose as towers, proud and tall,
Their chants rehearsed in hallowed hall;
They named the sun, yet felt no flame,
They drew the dawn, yet dreamed the same.

For knowledge, void of sight, is vain,
And scriptures read bring little gain,
If hearts are veiled, in shadows caught,
Truth fades to dust, on mere borrowed thought.

But should the blind receive the sight,
Then doubt dissolves in dawn's pure light;
So too the soul, when grace draws near,
Awakens from the sleep, and the truth is clear.

From the seed of one, creeds and sects grow apart,
Where each one bears a colour of the heart;
They battle on and on, with a holy claim,
Yet quarrel for a nameless name.

For verses bent by human pride,
Became sharp swords on either side;
But when the truth's ray breaks through the deep,
The streams shall flow, where the treasures are kept.

Then scales fall off, the veils are torn,
No soul needs to fight, no faith forlorn;
O' Lord, Thy light shall heal, and shall stay,
And night dissolves in the endless day.

So pour Thy fire through flesh and bone,
That we may shine as not our own;
To drink the glow, to live the breath,
And walk with Thee through life and death.

69

Dying Every Moment

From first drawn's breath to final veil,
The body hastens, in frail, to frail;
Each moment dies, though all unaware,
And we die in fragments, as thin as air.

Deeds in shallow may seem as gold,
Yet drains the lamp, as its fuel is sold;
Spent on illusions, vain, and untrue,
That can't hold, yet still pursue.

The tender frame, from womb once borne,
Blooms into strength, in beauty sworn;
But time will carve its furrowed lines,
And bind the heart with coils of thine.

Desires, perhaps the devil, silent and sly,
Entangles all, yet lets all to die;
The mind still dreams of endless flame,
While dust reclaims the boast of name.

Life is a bucket drawn from height,
It's stream a gift of sacred light;
But restless hearts, through rusty holes,
Let the holy waters slip to the shoals.

When the rope winds tight, the draw is done,
The vessel emptied, the grace hast run;
Though at start it brimmed with heaven's rain,
It yields at last to thirst and pain.

And when men, in sorrow, patch in haste,
But pierce new holes with every taste;
Till the shadow wins, and sparks decay,
And counting drops, as they fade away.

Yet still the stream stands, full, untrod,
Its depth the dwelling place of Existence;
If only the lust would turn aside,
To drink from stream that does not hide.

70

The Whale-fall

The sovereign of the surging seas,
With silent might and gentle ease,
Glides vast, a wonder few can name,
A moving temple, crowned in flame.

But when life's tide begins to wane,
It leaves its kin, the pods, the terrain;
Drawn by a call no eye can see,
It sails towards eternity.

It leaps in hymns of unseen joy once more,
Each plunges a holy psalm, each rise an eternal score;
Until the sea itself extends its arms
Where its song and breathing comes to an end.

Downward it drifts in holy sleep,
A banquet for the roaming deep;
Sharks and shadows, small and great,
Feast upon its noble weight.

Upon the floor, its bones remain,
A reef where life is born again;
From a giant's fall, new gardens unseen rise,
An alchemy that never dies.

Thus does its death outshine its birth,
A hymn to life, a gift to earth.
But man, when shadows round him close,
Clings to the lamps that only care.

We all are born without any plea,
Breathed into a being, wild and free;
Yet squander breath on illusive need,
While thirsting roots forget the seed.

O' man, behold the whale's descent,
It's yielding vast, it's death well spent;
In giving all, it gains the whole,
A quiet crown, perhaps a deathless soul.

71

The Runners

We are but sprinters on a fleeting track,
Chasing the wind with dust at our back;
Yearning for fames that wither and fall,
Yet missing thy breath that is deeper than all.

Applause may swell for the outward deed,
But the soul lies hungry, still in need;
Like pilgrims through sacred lands, who roam,
Forgetting the path, the truth, and thy Home.

Still they run, with blinded eyes,
Mistaking the world for the ultimate prize;
Yet truth whispers soft: ye are more than muddy clay,
Not fire nor air alone, but an eternal ray.

For earth, fire and water, and the boundless skies,
Are but mirrors of what within us lies;
All are the whole, though clothed apart,
Where the vast eternal lives within each heart.

Seasons will shift, and banners decay,
The crowds disperse, their cheers fall away;
But beyond the race, a meadow is spread,
Where victory and loss alike are dead.

There waits the joy untouched by strife,
The still, eternal, unmeasured life;
Where the runner lays his burden down,
And wears no garland, and seeks no crown.

72

The Dance Beyond Battling Life

The life is termed as a burdened strife,
When man chases peace in crooked ways.
From a cradle bound in chains of blaze,
He feeds the fire that burns his days.

The crown of self is thorns of grief,
The greater worn, the deeper grown.
O' weary man, thou drink the venom in vain,
Whilst nectar waits, yet left unseen.

The swollen self makes kin a foe,
And wars against the existence of song;
Awake as this path no man may win,
Defeat is sealed ere the march is long.

Step forth beyond the grasp of pride,
Rest in the waters still and deep:
See the flowers bloom without any request,
See the winds that turn, yet sow no reap.

The trees bow low through drought and flood,
The birds give praise with every food;

Their mirth declares, their dance proclaims:
"Awake, O' man, from the dreams of death."

All walk this earth by no desire,
All die unasked, the same attire;
Between these gates lies but only breath,
A shadow span that ends in death.

Whilst man wrestles in own chains of shade,
Existence feasts all where merry is made;
If unbound by desires, by mind, the life perhaps free,
A song resounds where truth is found as mystery.

When ego falls, love rains as light,
A drop more vast than star or sea;
It bids thee move with the cosmic tune,
To move in harmony with Thy tune.

73

The Painter of the Sky

In the calmness of silence, in stillness deep,
The self awakens from its sleep,
As a mote of vapour, frail yet bold,
It climbs the heights in arcs untold.

Upon the canvas vast and free,
Where stars are whispers of eternity,
It drifts, it soars in a patterned flight,
Yes, swift as flames, but soft as light.

Thou singest songs no ear can hear,
Yet clouds and stars dance as disciples near;
The winds obey the sovereign art,
And paint the horizons from Thy heart.

O' the Sculptor veiled in silence, unknown yet near,
Do our shifting shades obscure the 'love clear'?
Grant me the draught from the secret stream,
That I may fade into the eternal dream.
For hearts that soar to seek the grace,
Behold Thee throned in the silent space;
A thunderous voice, though silent and free,
Declares: "All streams return to Me."

And this fragile mote takes its part,
A note, a breath of Thy vast art;
As a tint upon the eternal skyline,
Yielding wholly to the unseen Divine.

And when the heavens thunder loud,
I may be the flash that rends the cloud,
A living echo through the endless skies,
Thy hidden voice that never dies.

At last to fall and embrace Thy endless sea,
As a drop reclaimed by eternity,
To rest as a dot in silence deep,
Till Thy command shall stir from sleep.

74

The Bamboo's Whisper

A bamboo sprout within my room did grow,
A token of love for the earth below,
I gave it food with tender hand,
Yet barred the sun it could not withstand,
It paled to yellow, its lesson plain-
Life bows not to comfort, nor to man's domain.

How oft my soul, in shadow's cast,
Has fed on mischiefs from ages past,
Chasing delights that swiftly fade,
Turning aside from the light that won't fade.
But in the void, where silence sings,
I learn to open my heart with wings,
To welcome beams that pierce the night,
And guide me forth to freedom's light.

There may I stand, though small, though one,
A tiny breath in the cosmic Sun,
A trembling note on an earthen string,
Awaiting the command to sing.
I seek not joy, nor dread the morrow,
I ask no crown, nor borrow sorrow.
But if Thy whirlpool draws me near,

Peace shall flow, love shall appear.
O' Light that shines through the shadow's veil,
The truth alone shall never fail,
As the bamboo bends yet does not break,
So shall my soul Thy likeness take.

75

The Single Creed of Truth

All are born to the rites of creeds,
Fed by customs, shaped by needs;
From the cradle, trained to march in time,
Yet blind to the source, deaf to the chime.

Like sentries bound to a parcel of clod,
Guarding their mud as though it were God,
They clutch the dust with fervent breath,
And boast of the weight of their fleeting death.

Life revolves through birth and grave,
As a tide on tide, a wave on wave;
Each return strips the built mask and the name,
Caste and crown dissolve into the same.

The glories fade, the battles fall,
Their echoes are lost in a silence of all;
Yet mankind clings to the shadows deep,
And dreams of peace that none may keep.

From spark to spark the journey bends,
The might unseen behind its path attends;
While truth stands clear in the living light,
The mind still gropes in self- made night.

There is but only one religion true,
Woven in grass, in air, in star, in dew;
No flag divides, no caste nor creed can reign,
As all are one in the vast domain.

And man, though lost upon the heights of knowing,
Still treads the paths where Thy light is flowing;
All willing hearts shall find the flame,
The hearth eternal whence all came.
No creed remains, nor banners fly,
All names and nations fade and die;
What is void shall endure, yet nigh,
The truth alone shall never die.

76

Withering Leaves Inspire

In autumn's rush, the leaves descend,
Their golden sighs to earth they send,
A hymn of thanks, a soft release,
That roots may drink and bloom in peace,
Their fading flames the sky adorn,
Their bareness shows the tree reborn,
Awaiting but Thy whispered breath,
To weave new robes from winter's death.

The leaf lives brief, yet sings of time,
Its colours chime in transient rhyme,
Does it recall its tender birth,
The morning sun, the toil of earth?
Or drifts it free, unbound, unflawed,
As a dancer lost within Thy laud?
Whilst man, unlike leaf, in chains remains,
Holding past flashing joys, rehearsing the unseen pains.

Yet are we not as leaves of Thee,
Hung on a vast and ageless tree?
The winds of yesteryear are gone,
The shadows fade, and the light moves on,
The dawn returns though night is deep,

The barren branch wakes not in grief,
The silver rains will descend, the sun will rise,
Yet man doubts still his very skies.

So cast away the husk of pride,
Let ego's brittle shell subside.
Fall as the leaf, released, forgiven,
To rest within the breath of heaven.
And when all shadows stripped have been,
The soul shall stand in living green,
Bearing fruits in season's play,
To light the world with love's pure ray.

77

The Roller of Thy Play

The coaster winds through air in game,
A breathless rise, a plunging flame;
Its curves embrace both thrill and dread,
Its heights exalt, its drops strike red.
Each quick turn, each fleeting flight,
Binds souls together in shared delight;
Till journey's end, no rest is found,
Yet awe resounds in every sound.

So too is life, a hidden art,
Where unseen tracks weave where shadows start,
We quake at plunges swift and deep,
Yet know Thy care the web does keep,
A mesh of stars, spheres spinning fast,
Beyond all thoughts, too bright, too vast;
Yet still Thy chariot curves the skies,
Where struggle sings and joy replies.

The heart that trusts need to fears no fall,
For the divine pulse sustains it all;
The drop perhaps a flight in disguise,
The tear, a jewel in wisdom's eyes;
Through every loop, through night and day,

The soul learns peace within the play;
And seeing the Unseen in each surprise,
It soars far beyond where terror lies.

Each peak dissolves, each valley flows,
The path unknown, yet still it shows;
Whether soaring or roaring, diving high or low,
It is the play, the breath, and the glow.
Ride on, O' soul, with a boldness free,
Let fear and longing cease for free;
And when the track at last is done,
To step off in peace and Thy will is won.

78

The Race of Shadows

In youth, we're driven to the race,
By crowds that press with blind embrace;
We chase for names, for dreams untrue,
Each step a theft from what we knew;
Like tumours creeping through the soul,
False fires drain and take their toll;
And life, untethered from truth's own way,
Is lured to the dark circles of decay.

They crown the muscle built of lies,
They guard the chains that none despise;
While dreamers bow to hopes of gold,
That slips through the hands which cannot hold;
Yet all they take, all they defend,
Will fall to strangers at the end;
For death still waits at every earthen hut,
And ends the grasping hand of the bait.

No covenant of dust shall stand,
When truth commands with sovereign hand;
The falsely built towers shall surely fall,
The real and true alone survive it all;
And many, longing to be free,

Change faiths like garbs of vanity;
From one cage to another, they shift in turn,
Yet still more inner chains they earn.

Religion's path was carved to lead,
Towards truthful light, the only seed;
Yet now it serves as tribes at war,
Where banners flare and egos soar;
What healing comes from such delusions?
When trade of faith sows more confusion?
The wiser soul tends still and near,
The silent core it holds sincere.

For truth belongs to none but Thee,
It blooms in every dot of cosmos trod;
From heart to throne, from star to clod,
It sings through stone, it breaks the rod;
The heart still hums a hidden song,
A peace forgotten, deep and strong;
While men still race on shadow's track,
The flame of ego burning black.

Till ash is loosed upon the skies above,
The wreck of all that man prized more;
When selfish fires consume the earth,
Where truth lies, masked beneath their mirth;
Yet for sure the souls at last should rise,
And see the world through their revived eyes,
One earth, one kin, one creed, one flame,
And One God who whispers every name.

No false beams then could lead any astray,
No shadows shall snare the heart to slay;
The soul would step into its core, the home,
Where cosmic fields in silence roam;
And wisdom, blazing like early rays of the dawn,
Would crown the highs, new and the worn.
A single hour, that is divinely sown,
Never before, and never known.

79

The Mirror's Secret

A mirror holds images, then lets it slip,
It keeps no shape, it keeps no flip.

The mind reflects, then casts away,
Yet one form departs, another stays.

It weaves its masks in colours bright,
It feeds the greed's thirst, it fuels the fight.

For king or beggar, gold or clay,
Are but reflections, all bound to decay.

When nothing stands, the mirror is clear,
A tranquil face of mind - no thought, no fear.

It whispers sharp, a voice unknown:
"All the grasp dissolves, and thy hold no throne."

Yet a few will see the glass so silent,
All chase the lights that never last.

Be as the mirror - still in watching, unmoved,
As the dream dissolves, the Self is proved.

80

The Unseen Horizon

Like travellers walking firm in faith, unknowing where the path may bend,
They follow guides in faith alone, not knowing where the road will end;
Yet the true horizon lies not far, nor on the plains where any feet have trod,
But deep within thy silent heart, lies Thy throne and footprints spread.

The flesh, a cage that binds the mind, still drifts with hungers, and all heed the call,
Yet hidden sleeps the unseen flame, awaiting to rise and to burn them all;
For life's simple care and crown is to be awake, and to know the self as whole;
Yet many, like fair Narcissus, who lost the pearl for thy beauty, in gazing at the bowl.

We are the life, the truth, the breath, the luminance of the boundless spheres,
The cosmos breathing in our breath, its rhythm pulsing through light years;
Why chase the far and faithless, when all the stars the

soul could enfold?
Why seek the fruit that bears no seed, when life's own seed is within thy hold?

Perhaps pride lifts many to lonely peaks, where no warm hand can reach or stay;
Their thrones are built of mind-born dreams that the truth will swiftly sweep away;
They sleep amidst a flashy, shaky world, and deaf to the whispers of the silent stream,
Blind to the might that moves through all, the source and substance of any true dream.

Awake to cast off the chains of night, and hear the voice that sings within;
The cosmos dwells in ye entire, the endless sky beneath thy skin;
All forms of dust, all realms of thought, will fade like mist at the dawn's breath,
But Thee remains, forever whole, the Force beyond all change, life and death.

81

The Touchstone of Truth

Gold, the shining lure of man, adored for glitter, sought for gain,
Is shaped in many cunning forms to charm the heart and cloud the brain;
Yet not all gleam is proof of worth, as its soul must stand the sacred test,
Where purity is weighed in fire, and dross is stripped from what is best.

Few can claim the goldsmith's art, to judge the ore with steady hands;
Yet for the one who knows the stone, the truth is clear, the verdict stands;
A simple mark upon its face will show the pure and expose the base,
And teach the eye to see beyond the lure of shine, the misty mask of the face.

So runs the world: all chase the bright, from crowns of power to heaps of gold,
Yet seldom seek the core of things, where purity is rare to hold;

Be wise before the leap is made, test well the heart, discern the soul,
For only truth, like perfect gold, is worth the weight, is wholly whole.

The world will count its glittering store, yet miss the jewel none can buy,
Forgetting a hidden gem, that makes the spirit never die;
Awake, and let that jewel rise, to taste its light is eternal breath,
To turn this earth to a sacred ground, and seal the grave of empty death.

The scrolls of old in holy hands hold the blades to polish the wisdom's stone;
Yet men may twist their edge aside, to cut away from truth alone.
But should the stone be rightly touched, it shines to show the just and truth,
Revealing in this tainted world the rarest souls, the purest few.

82

The Nectar of truth

In faith, many plead for the signs, for miracles to serve the desire,
They chase the glitters of the world, illusions lit by fleeting fire.

They love the joy, but flee the pain, and dream of bliss in realms above,
Yet perfect trust will fill the soul with silent strength and boundless love.

A grain of doubt, though small as dust, can spoil the feast the heart hast made,
And many name it demon's hand, when faith's hope of light begins to fade.

Yet doubt is but the shadow cast from minds that chase the phantom's call,
Unreal its shape, yet real its wound, that steals the peace and binds us all.

Where trust is mixed with false desire, the gold will dull, the flame will dim,
And seasoned generations may repeat that hollow song, the faded hymn.

But once the soul has drunk the cup, the nectar of pure trust remains within,
It anchors deep, beyond all the storms, where earthly scourge cannot begin.

There, in the depths of boundless void, untouched by grief, by greed, by shame,
The play remains immaculate, the truth forever stands the same.

83

Sailing Beyond Desires

Many sail on holy boats, drawn to a paradise they've heard before,
Yet cling to worldly egos, and stay where they first commenced;
They dream of radiant realms unseen, as ancient sages once described,
Yet the fetters of desire bind them still, missing the tiny flame inside.

From birth to death, the hunger grows, twisting all through every thought,
Perhaps their heaven's skies are shaded by the wishes they have sought.
The temple shines, the hymn rises, the smell of incense fills the air,
Yet all is lost if longing hides in secret corners of their living despair.

As thirst unquenched shall rise again, though nectar touches their lip,
The restless mind will reach again, and all may miss the gift from worship.
The soul must join the cosmic dance as an empty pot, a

silent flame,
Beyond the forms of thoughts, beyond the traps that wear the truth's name.

Beware of masks the mind may weave, the subtle traps to lead all astray,
Perhaps only a stillness, vast and deep, can aid the seeker on their way.
Release the chains the self has forged, let the dreams of ego pause to cease,
Step into the boundless void, the timeless ocean of infinite peace.

Then bliss shall bloom in a radiant glow, a flame no mortal tongue can tell,

Where joy is freed from grasp and fear, and truth in silent emptiness dwells.

O' soul, sail not in circles blind, but cast aside the cords to unbind;

For in surrender shines the pearl, the unknown Shine all seek to find.

84

An Awakening From Thoughts

Count from the countless thoughts that sweep the air,
How many are our own, and how many shall we bear?
Some softly accepted like whispers at dawn,
Most planted by mind when the guard was withdrawn.

They settle like seeds in the soil of the mind,
And bloom without any quests, their roots complex and intertwined.
And we wander through the gardens we never have sown,
And mistake their strange blossoms as fruits of our own.

Some entered by stealth through the cracks in thy trust,
Some hammered by voices of demand that ye must.
We bowed to the winds we thought were our own breath,
And drank from the cups that were tainted with death.

Yet deep in the heart, though its embers grew dim,
The flame still recalls its origin's hymn.
It called through the fog with a whispering cry,
Though ages passed in sleeping, it would never die.

Then came the surrender - not a loss, but total release,
The love in letting go, born of a thirst for peace.
The shadows fell back, and the captive now free,
The chains were but dreams, and the jailer was thee.

My soul looked once more through my eyes,
The truth was ever present beneath the skies.
What blazed in my heart at birth's first breath,
Now crowned the heights with colours of truth.

Twilight burned with a marvellous glow in fire,
A splendour no earth-born thought could inspire.
The sky became a mirror clear, of Thy truth,
The self I lost was the self untrue.

85

The Dance of the Morning Wings

At dawn I came to earn my sweat, the air still damp, the earth still new,
When black drongos rose and fell in arcs, with the glistening drops of dew,
The rooftop, wet from evening's rain, lay dressed in pools that caught the light,
While early beams of newborn sun bathed every leaf in green delight.

The starlings lingered at the edge, to sip the drops with patient grace,
As I, absorbed in laboured breath, beheld their slow and sacred pace.
A coucal watched with burning eyes from branches swayed by gentle breeze,
While drongos danced in sudden flights, as though to speak in signs to me.

Perhaps they hailed the coming rains that waited hidden, near at hand,

Or they praised the morning's gift, in tongues I scarce could understand.
May be, swift as hunger's call, they chased the mayflies through the air,
While I, in sweat, sought some part of their unbridled, holy fare.

Then came the bulbuls, red of cheek, to twirl a moment in the round,
Their soft steps stirred the starlings too, who took the stage without a sound.
A green barbet swept quickly past, intent on peanut's promised taste,
Yet none disturbed the morning's hymn, nor marred its joy, nor made it haste.

All moved as one - no claim, no fear, no thought to bind, no greed to sway;
Each played the part that day had set, in harmony with the dawn's own play.

86

The Vision Beyond the Cane

We think we know the blind man's path - how hard his steps, how deep his night,
He moves by sound, by gentle touch, bereft of vision's guiding light.
A cane becomes his faithful friend, a staff to read the earth's design,
Each step a trust, each pause a prayer, in patterns silent yet divine.

He knows not what the sighted praise - the painted sky, the meadow's hue,
Nor dreams the colours dawn may weave, nor shades that spill from evening's blue.
The rose for him is breath alone, its fragrance carved upon the air,
Its crimson face forever veiled, though countless eyes find beauty there.

But if, by grace, a dawn should break, and eyes long closed be opened wide,

What trembling wonder shakes his frame when floods of colours pour inside?
The tree, the stone, the passer's face, the sky stretched vast from east to west,
All surge like floods through his soul, too strange to name, too full to rest.

At first, his heart may reel in fear, the storm of light too sharp, too great;
But slowly, as the shock dissolves, he learns the art of sight's estate.
The Painter's art he now can read, the hidden brush that shaped the clay,
And walks no more with the cane alone, but in the brilliance of the lighted day.

So too we wander in the dark, with canes of thought and habit's chain,
We touch the edges, never whole, and call the shadow worlds our gain.
We name as truth what the dream hast drawn, we chase the forms that shift and die,
Yet deep within the soul's own core, a hidden sun prepares to rise.

For there it waits, the treasure bright, the flame that no eclipse can bind,
The light that knows no dusk nor dawn, an eye eternal, clear of mind.
To find it is to drop the staff, the props of learning, creed, and lore,

And step beyond the fields of night, where blindness rules the heart no more.

Then life will shine in colours pure, not bound to sorrow, fear, or wrong,
A spectrum born of deathless fire, a silence deep, a boundless song.
And every soul, in waking whole, shall see what mortal eyes never knew:
The known world itself is but a veil, and love the light that pours through.

87

Open Up My Heart

Erase the gathered logics old, that cloud the heart and blind the eye;
Let truth descend in tears of joy, not measured by the reason's lie;
Desire may arm thy hand with fire, yet never teach the lips to kiss,
The peace that blooms where love abides, the crown of every soul's true bliss.

The hand that feeds with coins by day may raise the blade in secret nights,
But an emptied mind, in silence vast, will brim with gifts of truthful delights.
When peace and love from formless depth brim over in the grateful heart,
The frozen law of mind dissolves, and wisdom takes the nobler part.

Yet few will climb the shadowed wall to touch the bell at heaven's door;
And fewer still, when hearing chimes, will cross the threshold and explore.

For loneliness unknown will press so hard, and fear may bid the soul to retreat,
And mind, in terror of the Truth, will call its chains a shelter sweet.

But still the voyage calls, beyond thoughts as the rites and virtues taught,
Where steps must leave the beaten track, and trust must pass the gate of thought;
The path is narrow, silent and bare, a heart stripped free of pride, shall seek,
There resounds the hidden song, the play divine, the truth unique.

O' Lord, if this vessel must be broken in the play, let it break not in part,

That every fragment drifts to Thy sea, and silence gathers the empty heart;

For only what is broken gathers width, enough to carry Thy endless flame,

And only emptied lives can echo the hidden music from the flame.

And when the fire has done its work, when its flames glow with sacred gold,
The soul shall rise, as a winged spark, not bound by any forms of old;
The self once lost is self regained, no mask remains, no shadow clings,

The heart becomes a sounding harp that plays the tune of deathless springs.

It enters the cosmic dance, where stars and atoms weave one song,
Where every tear becomes a pearl, and every loss proves nothing wrong;
No "I" remains to seek or weep, no chain endures, no night is kept,
The door is crossed, the bell is rung, the soul awakens which once had slept.

88

The Song Spilt Over the Sky

What song the tiny motes of mist, in blissful bounce through heavens high,
Have sung in tones no ear has caught, yet all the world has felt drift by?
The trees and greens, in rustling mirth, have swayed in time to that pure hymn,
While birds and beasts, in prance and call, have joined the chorus, full yet dim.

The peaks bowed with gleaming crowns, their snows released in streams so high,
A gift of thanks to unseen hands that stirred their joy in morning's light;
The stars have spun in twinkling dance, in secret steps no time can bind,
All joining the silent tune that threads the vastness, undefined.

This grace, spilt over all the globes, the wise shall receive in holy flame;

It finds the one whose lifted hands in prayer are still, whose heart is tame.
Not one who hoards the ancient lines of praise or gain or fleeting fame,
But one who dives into the deepest depths, and offers thy soul without a claim.

Then shall ye rise to heights unknown, where divinity's bright gallop flows,
Where every cell is filled with light too radiant to oppose;
And all illusions fade to nought, dissolving into realms above,
Where all is swallowed in Thy truth, crowned in the eternal love.

This river then shall sing this song, the waters ringing silver clear,
The wind shall carry whispers soft, that tell the saints and seekers near;
For one who yields the self away becomes the voice in which the Eternal calls,
A flute of reed, a hollow pipe, through which the timeless music falls.

The sun shall spread its golden cloak, and robe thy path in endless day,
While moonlight strokes thy quiet brow, and crowns thy nights in tender sway;
The elements shall serve all the steps, but not as a king, perhaps a servant true,

For one who bends in perfect love becomes the bow that bends to Thee.

And when at last the song completes, no singer left, no ear to hear,
The hymn shall swell beyond the worlds, dissolving all the forms and the fear.
For all that was and all to come shall blend into Thy silent sea,
The one who sang, the song itself, and the listener, all taste eternity.

The hymn is written in breath of stones, in depths of oceans, in flames that rise,
Its echo reverbs on every soul that longs for home beyond and beneath the skies.
And those who are still the restless storm, shall find the anthem, vast, untold,
For silence holds the final note, where heart and cosmos both unfold.

89

Nothing At All But Thee

The paths of life, the endless strife, the struggles pressing day by day,
Are shadows falling on thy wall, to dissolve before Thy brighter ray.
The treasures grasped by fading hands, thy eyes that chase, all will decay,
Fall as a dust beneath the truth: for Thou art the bread, the light, the way.

The loves of flesh, the bonds of name, are not the love that lifts ye soul,
The laws of want, the chains of rule, are not the law that makes ye whole;
Desire's throne, the ego's games, are but a mirage doomed to fall;
When death's cold herald comes in sight, the flesh and thought are nought at all.

The mind, beguiled, plays toys of joy to hide its grief in veiled disguise,
While all draw near the certain dusk that blinds the proud, unready eyes;

One foot is set within the tomb from birth, the other follows near,
Yet dreams still blaze in twilight's dim, though the end stands waiting, stiff and clear.

O' seek the seed from which the bloom receives its fragrance, pure and rare,
Before the night descends too deep, before the dark consumes the air.
Entreat the heart to cast off greed, to rest in radiant, holy void,
Where all the bubbles break, illusions fade, and only Thy pure song is voiced.

In silken silence, serene, supreme, Thy hidden shrine begins to gleam;
There wisdom wakes to find the core, the secret pollen in thy dream.
The self dissolves, its wall undone, its brittle fears are held no more,
And death becomes a passing mist, while Life eternal floods the core.

Lo the air vast, the boundless sea, the fire that burns yet makes no scar,
Thou callest all for a journey in, beyond the edge of sun and star;
The dust of worlds, the scrolls of time, all gathered in Thy mighty hand;
The small, the lost, the broken ones, all are cradled in Thy command.

If fate allows this soul to run this course, until Thy gates I see,
Then all who crossed eternity, come and embrace me in the boundless sea.
For love shall weave us all as one, where singer, song, and silence meet,
And all is swallowed into the cosmos and beyond, a perfection so vast and sweet.

90

When The Universe Disappears

Half-asleep in the hush of worlds, where shadows drift and visions stray,
My lids resist the call of light, yet something stirs in a mystic sway;
A note unformed begins to rise, it strikes my heart's still, and hidden core,
And spreads an unseen aureole, inviting me through a secret door.

The trees breathe wonders into dawn, green tongues of light through trembling leaves,
The wind and sun exchange their tales, which mortal thought has yet to weave;
In tones that human eyes can't name, as the spectrum floods the waking air,
Declaring truths in silent signs, too vast for hearts that wait to care.

The river sings of hidden springs, the mountain hums of ages past,

The bird becomes a prophet's voice, proclaiming joys that cannot last;
Yet in their passing song and stone, I hear a deeper rhythm arise,
A thrum that binds the dust to stars, a pulse that beats through earth and skies.

The veil of time grows thin and frail, I glimpse the thread behind the loom,
Where every life is warp and weft, each joy a light, each grief a gloom;
And yet the weaver's hand is so sure, no thread is lost, and nothing misplaced,
The cloth, though torn in mortal sight, is whole within the Eternal's taste.

I see Thy might there in every form - in grass and stone, in star and flame,
In man of course, though men forget the cosmic fire from which they came;
A brightness once in silence sealed, before the primal forms took its wing,
Still hums within the cosmic egg, the womb of every living thing.

To live is not to flee the world, nor to leave its laughter, grief, or wine,
But walk awake through all it gives, and accept its gifts as wholly thine;
For any seed may wake or end, unmarked by time, unbound by anyone,

And when that seed of truth is found, it crowns the eternal bliss of man.

Then fade, as mists before the sun, when verity at last draws so near,
Until the universe itself, dissolves into thy silence clear;
Where only emptiness shall remain, yet that null is whole,
The boundless womb of light and life, the resting place for every soul.

91

The Timeless Art of Life

Luring longings weave their threads, with glitters spun
in dream's attire,
A ceaseless loom of want and grasp that feeds the breath
of selfish fire;
From envy's bite to pride's deceit, from lustful spark to
rage undone,
The strands of folly blind to bind the soul, till the night
obscures the rising sun.

Intoxications wear their veils; from gold, to drugs, to holy
flame,
From thrones of power, frail and proud, to reverence
raised in heaven's name;
Desire's scent, like luring lights, seduces hearts with
phantom gleams,
All drink, but thirst the more ye drink, to drown within
the hollow dreams.

All must hear, yet few will heed, the law that seals each
mortal breath:
No bribe of gold, no flakes of flare, can sway the strong
reach of death;

The famine spreads from sect to land, where truth is sold for painted lies,
And still all wait with gluttonous eyes, for some salvation from unseen skies.

Through restless toil, sleepless nights, ye chase respect to lose the way,
Till all what's left are weary bones, the ashes of a life's decay;
Some march on narrow paths of creeds, to seek a heaven far above,
Yet miss the fountain at ye heart, the hidden spring of endless love.

When death comes to knock on thy muddy hut, no key of wealth can bar by door,
The hands fall still as the race is done, the grasping mind can clutch no more;
Behind remain the gilded chains, the fading crowns, the things ye kept,
For only one remains from the two at last: a soul that woke or a soul that slept.

And lo, the void beyond the grave is not of fear, but for thy release,
The soul returns unto its fount, from whence the play hast begun, to rest in peace.
All the glitter fades away, the longing dies, the restless tide at last is stilled,
The void becomes the womb of Light, where bliss, love and fate are fulfilled.

92

A Few Rays From Rig Veda

Before the atoms of science stirred, before the forge of iron age was lit,
The Rig Veda sang its secret hymns, where ancient flares of wonders were lit;
The thirst of hearts was then as now, to pierce the veil, to break the wall,
To open every shuttered sense, and hear the One who whispers all.

Who knows the hour the answer comes, or from what realm its steps are led?
The near today may drift afar, as joy and sorrow share one thread;
Yet still the call resounds through time - "Awake, O' soul, the path is clear,
The wisdom of ages awaits - unfold thyself, the truth is near."

Two birds abide upon a tree - one tastes its fruits, and one simply manifests,
Like Eden's tree of knowing death, and life's own tree of ageless peace;

Most feast upon the fruit that fades, and walk the road where endings lie,
Yet a few will sit in lucid light, where life and truth are one on high.
The calf is blind, yet feels the tongue that swiftly opens its hidden sight,
As the mother draws it to the streams of milk, a love eternal, free of night.
Through threads of Thee the spirit moves, to lift the veils that cloud the air,
To drink the nectar of the soul, and to join the dance that ends nowhere.

The sun ascends, the clouds depart, horizons shift yet keep their flame,
The golden rays implore the mist to split, that all may share Thy flame.
In silence, sense the dance of stars, the turning wheels, and the woven spheres,
And hear the rhythm of sky, to erase the fog of ancient years.

When Atman's ever moving wave flows with the cosmic soul, vast and free,
The world dissolves into a spark that leaps and joins eternity.
Through yielding of the self to Self, through temple's fire and altar's breath,
All reach the shrine's eternal shore, where cosmos dies to conquer death.

This earthen pot, though made of dust, holds a flare no night can overthrow,
The mind may roam to form ten thousand suns, yet never where the soul longs to go.
When Atman knows the truth revealed, all seeking fades, all roads are done,
Dissolved into the truth of absolute reality - where wisdom, love, and light are One.

No death remains, no shadow stays, the fire is quenched, the thirst is still,
The self beholds the supreme Self, the heart aligned with Thy perfect will.
The cosmic song becomes the breath, the silence shines, the void is won,
And all returns, forever whole, to Paramatman - All in One.

93

From Clay to Sky

We call ourselves the wise of earth, yet to dust all return once more,
Desire's fire still climbs the frame, though flesh grows weak, and strength is poor.
With wrinkled hands we grasp the dreams, with weary lungs we chase the breath,
Yet miss the gifts that hide in grief, the veiled delights of life and death.

Beyond the clay that moulds the form, beyond the tracks of our own ways,
There burns a flame no night can kill, a light untouched by passing days.
It pulses deep through time long lost, it echoes forth to call the near,
And every path the sages trod dissolves in stillness, bright and clear.

Behold the body, frail with age, behold the mind with cunning snares,
Fall not into the flood of wants, nor bind the stream that freely fares.

For those who walk with steps awake shall find the
Manasa Sarovar's shore,
Where thirst is quenched, where peace unveiled, shall
hold the soul forevermore.

The summer sun may scorch the earth, yet trees give fruit
with patient grace,
The sky still pours its rain on all, though man complains
of want's embrace.
We eat the gifts of earth for free, yet blind, we curse and
cry of pain,
We miss the dance of earth and sky, the call to walk their
way again.

No sin abides within the shrine, no punishment, no
fame, no name,
The truth is pure, the formless verity, beyond all praise,
beyond all blame.
Step out of clay, step out of mind, step in where only bliss
is found,
Where love and duty shine as one, and all false glitters
sink to ground.

The flesh shall fade, the mind shall fail, the passing self
shall pass away,
But enter Thy holy emptiness where shrines unlit erupt in
rays.
There, every chain is burned to dust, lies are purged,
illusions cease,
And silence thunders into light, and restless striving melts
to peace.

At last dissolve into the sea, a drop unknown, unseen, yet whole,
No longer bound to flesh or sky, yet everywhere, the immortal soul.
The hidden flare, the secret spark, the silence vast the saints shall keep,
Forever shining, never dim, in stillness pure, in silence deep.

94

The Blissful Curse

The Sun:, molten in its endless blaze,
A furnace no earthly forge could raise,
Burns beyond the bounds of time,
Perhaps, a hidden guilt, a nameless crime.

The stars from dust and vapour rise,
Colliding flames in endless skies;
They whirl, they fade, they shine, they fall,
Thy play sustains a blissful torment on all.

Yet when the scroll of years is read,
The Sun shall rest, the stars lie dead;
And man, O' passing spark of clay,
Where shall thy soul be cast that day?

Dream not the next breath gentle, mild,
Nor heaven's gate with mercy styled;
Perhaps a star in torment hurled,
Or comet lost through fleeting world.

Therefore, yield while breath is a gift given,
Find the hollow, to walk to heaven;
Reap the light of passing sun,
Before millennial fires begin.

All sing and speak falters before the Formless,
Whilst an empty silence crowns the Divine.
The atom stirred by a secret breath,
Leaps forth towards the highest skies.

95

The Illusive Shore

The mind, a deceiver in its art,
Weaves false visions from the start;
A thousand mirages rise and fall,
Drowning the Centre's sacred call;
In gold and kin it bids all blind,
With unseen ropes that chain to mind.

Thoughts deceive, and doubts ensnare,
Draped in robes of seeming care;
Faith's bright banners, and charity's hand,
Yet hunger rules the core, an unseen command.
Crowds chase shadows, blind, untrue;
Who can trust the far, if not seeing the near?

Renunciation stands as a mountain high,
But witness life, and the climb is nigh;
Unveil the senses, taste the breath,
Drink Thy bliss, to outpace the death;
Run not like a musk deer chasing the air,
The scent seems to recede, though it is own and near.

Some lie buried in endless night,
Some still slumber, though bathed in dim light.

Awakening whispers to all, yet few have heard,
The rumour remains, truth a forgotten word;
Where mind is calm, Thy play is shown,
Where mind is bound, all dreams are blown.

Ego's palaces of gold to ashes fall,
Yet demanding desires consume all;
Not solitude charts the hidden way,
But the fragrance deep where the Centre stays;
From the inner well the secret flows,
In a hidden aura, Thy love glows.

Let wisdom's storm, the heights rend,
Let rivers of love through earth descend;
Let carbon's dust to diamond rise,
Refined in fire before Thy eyes;
Draw all into Thy holy void,
Where love eternal cannot be destroyed.

96

The Manasa Sarovar

There toll the bells within my heart,
Not wrought by hands, nor mortal art.
Forged in the furnace, where time was unmade,
Whose chime was the first that Silence laid.
They rise from truth more ancient than the flame,
Where stones were carved by the formless Name;
Whose echoes stirred the vast unborn skies,
And woke the stars where darkness lies.
And every wave of Thy boundless sea of eternity,
Breathes forth the hymn of Infinity.

They call the sage who walks in me,
A wayfarer lost in desert's spree,
Who bent to drink from fancy dreams,
Forgetting the well of eternal streams.
The writ strikes in both warning and grace,
A voice from the monk's first dwelling place.
It brooks no pause, admits no plea,
For it speaks in the tongue of eternity.

I turn within where corridors wind,
Cobwebs of vows long left behind.
Dust of mornings neglected lies,

Darkened years beneath veiled skies.
Yet louder the bells resound, and clear,
A blade of light cuts through the fear.
The hidden gate awaits the hour,
Buried deep in my own power.

Now comes the cleansing, fierce, complete,
For sands grow thin beneath my feet.
I walk alone, yet not apart,
For Thine is the hand that leads my heart.
I pour my joyful grief like incense flame,
My joy as oil to praise Thy name.
That mercy may cleanse, that love may rise,
Like silver ascending through starry skies.

Then suddenly the dust of ages falls apart,
And breath returns to silent walls of art.
The dawn without beginning breaks,
The wheel of endless ages shakes.
The heights, the depths, without an end,
The farthest shores together blend.
And treasure shines within my core,
A jewel concealed, yet mine before.

Here is the shrine, the blest shore,
The Manasa Sarovar - a soul's bright shore.
A lake of stillness, vast, untrod,
Where no self gazes, and none but God.
Its waters ripple not, nor part,
For no "I" remains, no clinging heart.
Its waters hold no star, no flame,

For all returns to the nameless Name.
Only the hush of a timeless breath,
The pause that lingers 'twixt birth and death.

Upon its banks I in silence stay,
Not idle, but waiting in a sanctified sway.
For the Voice shall come as it came of old,
Certain but unhurried, gentle, and bold.
It holds the key, it calls me near,
To pass the veil I once held dear.
And bind me fast from cords above,
In the radiant chords of eternal Love.

Keep me here where Thy dance is true,
And steps are endless, ever new.
Till Thy messenger breaks the final night,
And I vanish in Thee as a spark in light.
No ending now, no hour, and no breath,
For Truth alone has conquered death.
Then still shall fall the heart's last knell,
For its ringing has served, and I served it well.
In Thee completed, dissolved, I be,
The bells are silent - yet sing of Thee.

97

Mesmerising Beetles and Bees

Through the framed glass, I watched the sky,
The sun arose, the dark did die.
As a weary knight, the night withdrew,
Before the dawn in burning hue.
It's a battle lost, its colours bled,
On heaven's canvas widely spread.
And in that glow my spirit saw,
The truth of life, both deep and raw.

Beneath, the guava gently swayed,
Its blossoms, white in tiers, were laid.
Each chalice brimmed with a secret store,
Bearing the nectar, the Elysium did outpour.
Around them, beetles clad in black and gold,
In armoured ranks both bright and bold,
Yet fought no foe, nor claimed domain,
But feasted free on nature's gain.

Some yielded blossoms, stepped aside,
No envy burned, nor grasping pride.
While man in folly, fierce and blind,

Seeks conquest as the prime mind.
The sun's long fingers touched the tree,
And reached within my thoughts to me.
It showed the gulf, immense and wide,
'Twixt nature's law and human pride.

Then bees descended, drawn with grace,
The beetles yielded them their place.
No greed was shown, no blood was shed,
No hunger turned to rage instead.
But man for land his hands may kill,
And shed blood, though never hold it still.
He hoards his bread though full his store,
And claims his might, yet starves the poor.

O' Lord of immense mercy, hear our cry,
And teach our stiffened necks to bow.
Bend us toward Thy humble way,
Where peace and courtesy together sway.
Grant us the lesson from beetle and bee,
The law of life, in simple forms.
That we may drink, but wound no more,
And share the feast, the earth outpour.

98

Thy Hidden Shore

Lo, I beheld Thee, O Lord, in the humblest of ways;
Not in the glitter that mortal desire displays.
Thyself strip the mind of its counterfeit masks;
Thyself openest the path unto the heart's sacred tasks.
Lead me afar from the dazzle that tempts and deceives;
Turn us from pulpits where even the preacher misleads.
For the truth is not shouted aloud, nor clothed in disguise;
It dwells deep within, where the still pulses arise.

At the core lies the seed of the cosmic decree,
Ever whispering low, the Thathwamasi.
For ages, men wander in grasping the air;
Shaking the world, yet the cosmos is there.
The mind is a conjurer, weaving its play;
In rows of phantoms that steal hearts away.
Men weep for the fiction, they cheer for the dream,
Yet drift unknowingly in a shadowed stream.

Awake, O' soul, behold the infinite Might!
The radiance concealed from mortal eyes of sight.
It showers unseen in a fragrance rare;
It sings a note beyond the earthly air.

Dance to its rhythm, taste what it yields;
Drink without measure from its boundless fields.
For the vessel shall break when the end draws near,
And the whisper of truth shall strike sudden and clear.

Yea, the grace of the Lord is scattered and spread,
Yet men chase the shadows their own egos applaud,
O the Core of souls, reveal us Thy way;
Keep us in pastures by night and by day.
Guide us, O' Lord, to the crystalline shore,
Where Manasa Sarovar abide evermore.
There silence reigns, enfolding the deep,
And in that void, love and peace all shall keep.

99

The Dew Upon the Leaf

Like crystal dewdrops on the lotus wide,
They balance in poise on the trembling tide.
They gleam as pearls in the newborn light,
Casting their beams to the edges of sight.
The wind may stir, the waves may bend,
The mind laments, "This must not end!"
It clutches the drop as though time would yield,
Yet the secret within remains sealed.

Few taste the joy of the evanescent dance;
Most clutch the leaf as their only chance.
Blind to the gift of the present delight,
They barter the ride for imagined might.
For rise and fall are but passing turns,
The tide shall claim what the heart still yearns.
So drink of the joy while the day is fair,
Before the drop melts into the air.

Yet the droplets laugh at the jostling play;
They curse no wind, they bless no day.
In silent knowing they gleam and wait,
For the waters vast are their final state.
They shine as gems in the shifting scheme,

Born of both sorrow and joy's bright gleam.
From the seed of silence their birth is spun,
Radiant, they stand till the journey is done.

But when wrapped in the leaf's false shield,
The restless mind keeps its captives sealed.
Learn from the dew, how to ride with grace,
Unbound by chains of gain or disgrace.
Dissolve in the depths where no shadows creep,
Where the Unknown waits in silence deep.
There drink the nectar beyond all strife,
The sweetness distilled through life on life.

100

Into Thy Ocean and Beyond

Thy presence, our own true seed, yet so small,
But vast where cosmic currents call all,
The pulse that bids all the realms extend,
The truth where every birth must end;
The dance of unity sways through space,
Proclaiming might on every sphere;
Unknown vibrations and sights unseen,
The spectrum shines both old yet so green.

The scriptures flame, perhaps the sages pray,
Unveiling the formless, in silent ways;
They clear their inner that rends the veil,
Where mortal thoughts and measures fail;
Beyond the chants, beyond the creeds,
Beyond the rites, man thinks of his needs,
We crawl like worms on crusted clay,
Lost in the storm of our selves decay.

Like waves that boast a momentary reign,
Their shiny crests are brie, and in vain;
They lure the heart, they dazzle the sight,

Yet miss the stillness masked in the dark;
For when the drop returns to its base at last,
All foam and tide are shadows of the past;
Only the boundless depths shall remain,
Where truthful silence shall ever reign.

Within the drop the secret hides,
Till inner vision breaks what time divides;
It pours itself in the hallowed sea,
Where hollowness holds the infinity;
The witness stands untouched by name,
By joy, by grief, by shade, by fame;
Fragrant currents flood the whole,
Revealing eternity, the timeless, endless whole.

And in that glow the body shall still,
The mind shall dissolve where radiance spill,
The stream of brilliance, vast and untold,
Consumes the dream, that turns the dust to shiny gold;
Fearless, I drift where Thy hands may lead,
Past the skies, past the stars, past the mortal needs.
Till I get lost in Thy primal flame,
The energy none can bind nor name.

101

Thy Book Beyond Life

Days and nights flow like silver streams,
They slip away like swift moving dreams,
From breath to the dust, and from dust to flame,
They vanish back to whence they came;
Decades fade on the touch of a single breeze,
Centuries fall like withering leaves, so fast;
Time shall devour both the king and the throne,
And shall leave Thy seed to stand alone.

Time, the hand none dares to touch,
Yet rewrites the history in a retouch,
Where it steals our tongue, it dims our eyes,
It builds, destroys, and testifies as it goes,
Yet man still toys with the passing hours,
Still weave his garlands out of flowers;
Still barter pearls, yet for empty shells,
Still drinks the draught that illusion sells.

Yet deep within, the heart resonates Thy call,
A voice that breaks all mortal walls,
"Awake, O' sleeper, seek the flame,
The truth behind thy brief lifetime."
For time is short, and the robe is clay,

The shell will crack soon, the husk will decay;
Yet still the tiny wave must join the tide,
And dance in joy until all dances collide.

See the sparrow sings, the river flows,
The hidden seed of Thee, in silence grows,
The stone resounds, the wind proclaims,
The stars all whisper Thy holy rhymes,
The worm that crawls, the root below,
The silver moon above in a milky glow,
Each bears the pulse, the secret flame,
Each beats with the timeless rhythm, the same.

When emptied clean of all clinging ties,
The soul will unveil its inner skies;
It sheds the veil of the grasping hands,
It treads where truth alone still stands;
In Thy light and void the script is read,
Where all the living meet, and the dead are shed;
Where silence reigns and rest is deep,
Where time dissolves in an endless sleep.

Then wisdom breaks as a ray of fire,
And floods the soul with vast desire,
The body drinks the nectar so pure,
Its light remains within, forever for sure,
A rose unseen by mortal sight,
Its bloom extends through realms of space in light;
Its petals hum the song of the stars,
Its fragrance heals all ancient scars.

Its fragrance drifts through sods to sky,
Its pollen wakes the breath so high,
And in that bliss, all words are flame,
All sounds shall return unto the eternal name;
All rigid tongues melt into flowing streams,
Where minds dissolve in holy dreams;
Script and verse become a sacred song,
When the soul recalls where it belongs.

No limit can bind, no chain can hold,
The radiance from its hidden fold,
It bends all the paths of ancient time,
It sways the stars in course sublime;
Crowns are raised yet crowns are dust,
Nations bloom yet shall fall in rust;
But Thee who speaks through the silent flame,
Remains forever, all the same.

The wave returns, the drop is drawn,
No crest remains, no foam lives on;
As the ocean claims its wandering marks,
And folds that spark within the deep.
What seemed to rise, what seemed to fall,
Was the one, vast flame, that bound it all;
The sea and drop are not apart,
The self and Thee are all one Heart.

And when at last this frame shall end,
And as a grain of dust to return in gain,
No fear shall bind, no shadow stay,
For Thou shalt wilt fold my soul away;

The stream of brilliance, vast and untold,
Take on the dream that turns dust to shiny gold;
What once was mine was always Thine,
Yet what Thine was ever, still is mine;

102

The Narrow Path of Life

The short life upon this circling earth,
A trial so deep, of hidden worth.
No crown of gold, no mortal name,
Can bind that law, nor quench that flame.

It weighs the heart by secret light,
Refines the soul through day and night.
Through joy and grief, through events and years,
The pilgrim climbs beyond all his fears.

The laurel fades, the crowd is gone,
What worth the applause where truth is none?
The jewel within, untouched by rust,
Alone remains when all is dust.

Who knows what roads thy spirit trod,
What forms it wore in commands of God?
The sage, though clothed in mortal breath,
Still bears the marks of life and death.

All woven joys, all passing pain,
Are masks that fall, no part shall remain.
For death reveals the greater way,
For the seed concealed, the hidden ray.

A day shall rise when wrath is still,
When pride is gone, when love is will.
No sword shall strike, no envy stay,
But peace shall crown the endless day.

Yet few will walk this narrow road,
Where none may share another's load.
The path is carved in secret stone,
The strength to tread is thine alone.

And when at last the journey ends,
No fear remains, no self defends.
The drop returns into Thy vast sea,
The soul is One, the soul is free.

The play is closed, the scroll is sealed,
The heart unveiled, the light revealed.
And Love alone, the timeless flame,
Forever dwells, beyond all name and time.

103

The Hymn Beyond The Veil

In shadow's keep the weary lie,
They clutch to breath, yet still must die.
They trade the peace of gentle rest,
For chains of pain that choke the breast.

What gain is won in grasping breath?
What loss is found in life or death?
The veil conceals the riddle's sum,
The end that waits for all to come.

The clock forgets its course at last,
The thief arrives, the gate is passed.
The flame is blown, the hand is stilled,
The mortal lamp no longer filled.

Yet mortals plead to stay the hour,
To hold the sand, to thwart its power.
But if there is no end to close the chase,
Then life will bind in endless pain of race.

For death relieves the pains of night,
It clears the field, it lifts the blight.
It opens gates unseen no hand may bar,
And leads the soul where wonders are.

The clay is loosed, the soul takes wing,
It finds no loss nor pain, but gain to sing.
The tears are pearls, the wounds are gold,
As the mourn breaks forth, the night grows old.

Death is no end nor void, no final stand,
But the servant of a higher Command.
It leads beyond the fleeting breath,
To a Love that conquers even death.

104

The Pilgrimage of the Soul

From the silent womb where pulses deep,
A soul awakes from its hidden sleep;
Through muffled destiny it stirs into light,
To burst out into the mortal sights;
It walks the span in a rush, from first to last,
Through trials deep, through futures lust;
Through joy and grief, through toil and pain,
The path designed for all wandering men.

Yet many dream in shadows in vain,
They chase the dust, and they clutch the chain;
They drink the mirage in the sand,
And lose the treasure in their hand;
For innocence they cast aside,
And from the pulse of truth they hide afar;
But all that glitters shall fade away,
Like fancy lights at the break of the day.

The mind's proud towers cannot stand,
They sink like ships on storms so sad;
The banners fall, the empires drown,
The seeds of pride as ashes burnt;
But the wise shall see the passing show,

As clouds that drift, as winds that blow;
For always the truth within remains the same,
As silent fire, a silent spark, all the time.

To walk as a man is no small test,
The pilgrim seeks, yet finds no rest;
In births and deaths, through grief and flame,
Through passing time that ends the same.
But all the sleepers shall rise at last,
Their masks shall fall, their night be past;
Where love shall call, and peace be heard,
With voice as soft as a twilight humming bird.

Raise not for me a tomb of stone,
Nor a deck with wealth, what time will own;
For storms shall strip and winds shall tear,
And leave no trace of the relic made there.
Awake instead into the Light's vast sea,
Where all dissolves, yet all is free;
Where body fades, where shadows flee,
And soul returns forever to Thee.

105

Where Art Thou

Perhaps the face of God we trace, is carved by human hand,
In manly moulds, in worldly ways, in forms that all can understand;
As a shadow cast of greed and fear, on the heaven's boundless skies,
Yet Truth beyond all measure dwells, unseen by all mortal eyes.

Perhaps in mortal thought we frame the Lord in manly guise,
With strength adorned, with crowns of gold that dazzle fleshy eyes;
In worldly pomp our fancies turn, to thrones of revere and its fame,
Yet are shadows only that veil, the Truth that none on earth could name.

None hath truly seen the Eternal, Thy face is hidden from mortal gaze,

Illusions rise as drifting veils, clouding the soul in countless ways;

How shall the Formless be grasped by thought, when
thought itself is bound by clay?

Perhaps misreadings through the ages have led the seeker's
heart astray.

The sages sang, the seers proclaimed, yet none Thy form
ever found,
For Thee who births the worlds, dwell in an unknown
silence so profound.
No shape can bind Thy endless Might, and no ornament
nor praise can define,
The might of God is formless still, so eternal and too
divine.

Thus let not pride of manly strength measure Thy reign,
Nor the glitter of futile thrones or robes, all perhaps in
vain;
Thou art in all, in every living breath, in whispers soft
and true,
For the wise to sense and act, for thy soul's revival, just
and due.

106

The Looming Solitude

Alone we come, alone we go,
No crown, no coin, no mortal show,
The silent shore always awaits us there,
Where shadow folds in patient prayers.

One dawn I heard a fisher's song,
His hands were worn, his path was long,
A sacred call through the fog and frost,
To summon the light when hope seemed lost.

Perhaps to guard the creeping fear,
That stalks his heart when none are near,
Or to remind his wandering soul,
That even silence keeps it whole.

Yet many flee the naked truth,
They wear the masks, they chase the youth,
Of fleeting dreams and hollow praise,
Blind to Thy gaze through night and days.

They seek the gates of heaven so high,
While hell's imagined shadows lie beneath.
Yet every breath, unseen or unheard,
Is caught and held within Thy cloud.

Fear not the veiled, but the boundless Real,
Nor to dread the realms the flesh can't feel,
For even now a tiniest spark,
Reflects the Light that birthed the dark.

In the hush of night, in the blaze of day,
Thy subtle tremor shall guide the way.
No fear, no loss, no mortal binds,
Hide not the One that all souls shall find.

So wander deep, yet rest in grace,
Through veils of time, through space's face.
Each breath a step, each step a prayer,
Each silence hums Thy presence everywhere.

107

The Invitation of the Stars

The stars invite with silver gleam,
Yet truth is near, not far in dream.
The mind pursues the distant desire,
And misses close its true fire.

The cosmic waltz through endless night,
Declares Thy word without a light.
Yet mortals, bound to passing days,
Ignore the song which existence plays.

The sun may rule its circling round,
But who shall name the Might profound?
Men chase the rim of boundless skies,
Yet pass their Heart before their eyes.

Creeds rise and sink like waves to foam,
No preach nor rite can lead ye home.
Yet leaf and stone the natures flow,
Proclaim the Source all hearts may know.

The moon ascends, the oceans swell,
The mountains bow, the forests tell,
Through all, an eternal pulse sustains,
The breath that runs in every vein.

Why chase the veil, why fear the night?
Whilst the nearest Truth is still and bright.
In dust, in flame, in breath we find,
The secret Cord that holds mankind.

When shadows fall and time is gone,
No crown remains, no deceiving throne;
Each spark returns, each soul shall claim,
Its rest within Thy deathless Flame.

108

Peace of Mind

"Peace of mind" as all mortals say,
A passing shard in thought's decay,
A fragment unseen of the restless tide,
But not the ocean where peace abides.

It grants a balm for momentary relief,
A veil to hide the deeper grief,
A silken mask on wounds unhealed,
Yet roots of the ache are still concealed.

Many wander, from sect to sect,
Seeking peace they can't protect,
Religions meant to lead to Thee,
The paramount, the timeless source.

All shifting cages, the freedoms frail,
Yet cannot grant the rest all hail;
They feed a few with hollow pride,
While dimming light on every side.

Perhaps clever to dwell in any creed,
If it's sacred heart that's what you heed,
Hold its flame both pure and sure,
And Thy love eternal shall endure.

They dream of peace in the hush of night,
Yet cradle thorns beneath every delight,
They write their tales in shadow's tone,
Where unrest comes and all is overthrown.

But true eternal Love, a still that flows,
Unbound by the mind, and no trade it owes,
It asks no grasp, it makes no claim,
It blooms beyond all illusion's frame.

Yet man pursues the fragment's glow,
To soothe their ache, to numb their woe,
They forget the greater phase that frees,
Where self dissolves in boundless seas.

O' man, drop the brittle shard,
Leap into Love, though path may be hard,
For there the soul shall find its release,
And drink from the endless well of peace.

As moon reflects the distant sun,
So 'peace of mind' reflects the peace,
A tiny flame, a mirrored dream,
A core from which all worlds still gleam.

The stars keep their watch in silent truth,
The seas repeat their ageless proof,
An endless call to rise, to sing,
To dwell where all true hearts take its wings.

109

Wings of the Unseen Breeze

From ages past, a bird in flight,
Has stirred man's heart towards heaven's height,
A secret fire within him awakes,
To seek the sky, and the bond it breaks,
Yet oft he knows not it is near,
The breeze that whispers soft and clear,
For the wise shall trace the hidden way,
Where souls may rise and hearts shall stay.

They wheel beneath the vaulted dome,
Unbound by the link, untouched by home,
No weight can mar their holy song,
The winds have borne their wings along,
O' learn the pulse, the breeze's art,
That stirs the soul and lifts the heart;
For first, the air must kiss the mind,
Before the eagle's heights we shall find.

Search deep within the earth and the sky,
Where treasures rest no eyes descry,
The beaming soft ray, the bird's soft hymn,

Unveils a love the winds have flown;
Yet closed are the hearts that will not feel,
Thy breathing pulses, so hushed, so real.
They miss the feast, the passing flame,
And cling but shadows in their name.

For love is like an unseen guest,
That moves the soul, yet leaves no dust,
The embracing breeze no eyes have ever seen,
Perhaps like the love that flows unseen,
It calls us forth, and bids pride depart,
And breaks all walls around our heart,
To carry us through to realms afar,
Beyond the reach of sun and star.

Till all dissolves without a seam,
Like a dew drop poured into the stream;
Where the wind, the wing and the sky are one,
And no mortal may see, for none has begun;
Here Love becomes the air, the call,
The rest, the flight, the mystery that rests in all,
No higher throne, no greater prize,
Than Love eternal, beyond the boundless skies.

110

The silence of the ancient banyan

Beneath the arms of a banyan vast,
I stood where roots like prayers were cast,
Where the hanging cords in silence spoke,
Of truths any worldly tongue bespoke,
The air was thin in earth's embrace,
A hush that stilled the hurried pace.

From branch to branch, the golden light,
Poured gently through the shades of night;
It touched a nest where fledglings swayed,
And hearkened to the sermon laid;
The banyan spoke, yet voiced no sound,
Its counsel pressed my heart unbound.

In a whisper soft, 'patience holds the storms,
Unseen the roots are, yet life it forms.
The shade that falls is never kept,
But freely o'er all the weary swept'.
And down a single leaf in spirals flew,
A silent truth the stillness knew.

It came to rest beneath my feet,
A seal for truth pure and complete;
And in that hush I heard the call,
From my root within, to yield to all;
Not upwards only must we grow,
But deep where hidden waters flow.

Till storms become a gentle song,
Docked with roots in peace all belong;
Till the soul itself, both vast and free,
Becomes the shade, becomes the tree.

And then I knew, in breath profound,
That all is the root, and all is the ground;
The leaf, the shade, the storm, and the sky,
In Thy play that never fades or cease.

111

The Hidden Chamber

Within the heart of man there is,
A secret chamber silently vibes;
Known by many, yet entered are rare,
The seed of light beyond compare,
A mirror of the Infinite, and so bright,
Cradled in stillness, pure, alight.

Through ages vast the seekers came,
To chase that vibe, without any name;
Yet few beheld its radiant gleam,
Returning transformed, as from a dream,
The rest still wandered, veiled in the night,
Blind to the chamber's inner light.

The multitudes who, in faith abide,
With tales of death within and realms outside;
They long for heavens taught in a deem,
For a paradise beyond the dreamy stream;
Yet the truth remains behind the veil,
Where mortal memory dares not to sail.

The restless mind, a sovereign blind,
Casts shadows on the mind's own shine;

But they who pierced its shrouded way,
Stood like Sun, at a day's noon ray,
Where all the shades dissolve and flee,
In the excellent brilliance of eternity.

Across the ages, all sages knew,
A wisdom remains deep, eternal and true;
No tongue could hold, no script can bind Thy art,
The radiance dawned within own heart.
To those unseeing ones all was shade that need a fill,
A breathless hush no word could fill.

112

The Root and the Honey

A spoon of honey tempts the tongue,
So bright and sweet, with praises sung;
It whispers for health, a life made long,
In its nectar's glow, in a golden song;
Yet what men taste is but a tiny flame,
A fleeting spark, without the name;
For Amruth flows, serene and divine,
When soul refines the heart's design.

The blossoms yield their fragile gift,
The bees in tireless labour to sift;
But blooms must fade, their sweetness fall,
No mortal petal can hold it all;
Only through a hidden alchemy,
The hive distils it to eternity;
And honey, wrought by the secret art,
Becomes the healer of every heart.

But whence begins this nectar's birth?
Not branch, nor leaf, nor stem on earth;
The root alone, in the dark soil concealed,
Drinks from unseen springs, that none revealed;
From depths unlit and unseen, it draws its power,

And crowns the life with buds, and the flower;
So too the man must downward go,
To seek the source and the roots we know.

In solitude's unmeasured peace,
Where trades and clamours find its release,
Where the holy emptiness shall descend,
A silence profound, where all the seeking shall end,
Yet most will flee its quiet calls,
And chase the noise that binds them all;
But few remain, and a few will see,
The silence that births eternity.

For there the unheard wisdom sings,
The breath of bliss on its unseen wings;
It moves like wind in a hidden glade,
A whispered grace that does not fade.
Whilst the body waits its turn to rust,
In the soil's embrace, by the earth caressed;
But the spirit shall drink a sweeter wine,
The honeyed draught of love divine.

Then they shall taste the nectar true,
Not from the bloom, but from the root's deep dew;
A sweetness that time can never bind,
The feast of saints, the Light refined;
The hermit's fire, the seeker's key,
The hymn of love and peace till eternity;
To drink the honey at its source,
And to join the everlasting course.

113

The Silence of the Summit

High above the valley's cloudy mist,
Where smokey veils through the air persist,
A lone peak stands in its quiet grace,
Its crown untouched by time or space;
It whispers softly to the wind,
The secrets that the ages pinned;
Breathing the same unbroken serene air,
The ancients knew, beyond all care.

From its hidden heart the streams descend,
Through stone and sand their courses blend;
They sing of life in its patient flow,
Of roots that drink, what skies bestow;
The Giver unseen, yet always near,
Feeds all that grows with silent cheer;
And life, in a humble reverence drawn,
Receives Thy gift from dusk to dawn.

Clouds wander past like monks in prayer,
Resting a while, then drifting where?
The mountain teaches weightless ways,
Of passing things, on sunlit days.
The art of release, the truth of still,

The letting go of all our will;
To stand unmoved in life's vast stream,
And hold the heart within its dream.

O' the unseen Vibe of the heights, arise,
Unmoved by the storm, unshaken by the skies;
Teach my soul to find its core,
To let the world's loud clamours pour,
Through an open mind like the pine swept wind,
And keep my inner light intact and undimmed,
The steadfast flame, serene and bright,
That shines unseen, yet warms my night.

And when my heart has scaled its height,
Where all the streams and winds are one in sight,
The peak, the cloud, the sky and the stone,
Become my soul, and all Thy own.
Unbroken, vast, eternal and free,
And my spirit breathe the Mountain infinite.

114

The Love beyond love

The love, the world proclaims, is so brief,
A momentary glow, a borrowed grief.
The Love eternal burns unseen,
Its light untouched by pride or mean.
What men call love, perhaps, is trade of acts,
Is but a shadow that distracts;
No bargain made of loss or gain,
Can hold the heart, can break the chain.

Like distant stars through veils of haze,
The world's love blurs the soul's own gaze.
Its vision dimmed by dust of need,
It crowns as 'pure' what feeds the greed.
Even fatherhood, and mother's song,
Hold threads of truth perhaps woven wrong.
The highest praise, the loudest acclaim,
Cannot contain Thy timeless flame.

Yet still, in love's proclaimed embrace,
Men chain, enslave, and strike apace.
Nations arm their sons for war,
Their neighbours suffer, near and far.

On this tiny globe where all hearts cry,
The eternal sky looks on, from most high.

True love flows forth from every cell,
It's fragrance free, no bond can quell nor kill.
It springs from depths, beyond the moods of all,
And plants its seeds where once feud was full.
To drink from this stream is to release,
The self, the grasp, the false caprice;
To rise and touch the boundless spring,
Where every heart becomes a spring.

So let us wake while breath remains,
And shed the shadows, and drop the chains.
For love in deeds alone is vain,
A fleeting shadow, not the love of Flame.
The purest love bears no name, no face,
Yet fills all space outright with silent grace.
It lifts the soul, unseen, untamed,
And binds the cosmos within its frame.

115

The Fisherman & the Line

A fisherman waits by the murmuring tide,
Casting his bait where the slippery scales glide.
He pierces a creature in a merciless art,
Blind to the wound he has placed in its heart.
Yet knows he not, on a hook of his own,
His mind is the line, and the bait is his bone.

Men opt their menus and boast they are free,
Yet dine at the table of fate's vast sea.
Each one a morsel in cycles untamed,
Each one a player, yet equally chained.
Feel for the baits that in anguish sway,
And ye will not harm it for profit or play.

The lion will strike when hunger is near,
But sleeps by the lamb when the night is clear.
The deer may dance in the predator's sight,
When bellies are full in the moon's calm light.
Some ancient mercy within them flows,
A wisdom the greed bound heart never knows.

Live and eat for thy living, but not lust,
For greed turns the hunter's bow into dust.

Rise above the cruelties hunger may breed,
And plant in today a gentler seed.
Let mercy guide each hand and mind,
And leave no trace of harm behind.

For each who casts is himself in the snare,
Each captor a captive, bound unaware.
And every bait in the waters of strife,
Dreams the dawn of a hookless life.
So break every line where sufferings spun,
Till no soul is a bait, and the hunt is done.

And when the tides of life flow calm and clear,
Each heart will know no shadow of fear.
The stream, the fish, the wind, the sky,
All merge as one, where hooks need no greed nor lie.
The unseen limitless law, eternal and free,
Becomes the fearless, the boundless sea.

116

The triggers for the Wise

World's course would not have ended so soon,
Had the wise not walked beneath the sorrow's moon;
Yet Siddhartha, pressed by the silent dart,
Awoke as Buddha, with an open heart,
Thanks to the hands, both near and dear,
Whose hidden strikes drew freedom near.

Like a spring, poisoned and shadowed at birth,
Corrupts the rivers that wind through earth,
So too the tender years, in worldly guise,
The fed bright dreams fading in dying eyes.
Yet from such tainted currents flow,
Unseen secret keys obtained, the awakened know.

Many will gather when fortunes swell,
And weave sweet tales all tongue may tell;
But when the vessel stands dry and bare,
The crowd departs, and none is there.
All such deeds, in false love traced,
Are scattered leaves the winds efface.

From ignorance blooms the mind's deceit,
Gilded in words, beguilingly sweet;

Yet once that mask in the light is caught,
It marks the soul for a pilgrim's lot,
To tread alone, with patient will,
The narrow road through the silent hill.

And know, betrayal is but the chisel's blow,
That shapes the form the mind will show;
The wound becomes the window wide,
Through which the light pours in to guide.
Thus pain, when read by a seer's eye,
Is the stamp of freedom the wise will see.
The sorrow of moon becomes Thy dawn's flame,
And loss is crowned with an eternal name.

117

Walking With the Dead

I trust no secrets nor screams but the Truth,
For man's frail tongue betrays the proof;
All I have seen so far, and all I have heard,
Bears imperfections in thought, word and deed.

The race of men, so blind, so vain,
Chasing shadows through dust and pain,
Proclaiming God with a doubting breath,
Yet wandering far into the jaws of death.

A few, unseen by the market's eyes,
Unheard where the clamorous traffic lies,
Stand as witnesses, calm, apart,
As stars untold, with a hidden heart.

They turn with the wheel that the cosmos spins,
Riding with the current where silence begins;
Beyond the boast of the worldly light,
They walk unseen through the endless night.

And I, a soul in this mad parade,
Stretch out my hands through the slot Thee made;
Starving to carve where Thy mercy streams,
Beyond the veil of these passing dreams.

Yet most know not the sleep they keep,
They walk with the dead, though not in sleep;
Mother by daughter, brother by son,
Yet none awaken, not even once.

In silence, true souls discern the face,
That hides beyond the blood and the name;
Each fading bond is a fleeting flame,
That leaves no mark but a borrowed name.

And nearing the waters, silent and still,
Where the vast horizon bends to Thy will,
The wise discern the false from the truth,
The dreamer vanishes from a soul made new.

As if in an ancient tale the ages weave,
Where dreamers wander, yet still believe,
Never knowing the flame they keep,
Till Light awakens their spellbound sleep.

118

The Unseen toil, Uncrowned

Man in elder days, the mother bore,
Her travail fierce, yet silence more;
Like a doe that labours in the shade,
Or a seal on ice where none have stayed.
Unwatched, unsung, her pangs were plain,
Yet life was born through hidden pain.

Yet now praises raised with banners bright,
With thousand voices, in loud delight;
Yet creatures all, both large and small,
Bear burdens deep without the call.
For trumpets sound where danger's none,
Yet silent labours go undone.

But the father stands as an oak in frost,
Roots deep, yet nameless, unseen efforts lost.
He braved the storm, he ploughed the field,
His bread and strength became the shield.
A pain untold, a joy of world denied,
Enduring still, though none beside.

What birth endures is but a span,
The longer toil belongs to man.
Yet garlands crown a moment's breath,
Where greater gifts slip into a birth.
Perhaps one will cross a sea to mourn,
But not thy street for lives forlorn.

In weaving vast, no thread is more,
Not mother, child, nor father's core.
Each placed by Thee that none may see,
That pulls the threads eternally.
Boast not, exalt not, but behold,
The snails' fight, the salmon's bold.

Yet modern tides let driftwood lie,
While vessels sail away and births pass by.
Each soul must face its voyage alone,
Beyond the shore, to currents grown.
Where the sea of Thee and own life blend,
The helm returns to Thee at the end.

119

The Star in The Skeleton

Be mindful always, of the crown you bear,
A silent constellation woven there;
A lattice of white, concealed from sight,
Yet burning within with eternal light.
At its heart, a star no time can bind,
A luminance from realms beyond mankind.

When ye cradle thy head, let wisdom show,
A moon of bone in its patient glow;
Orbiting the sun of the soul's great fire,
Drawing you upward, ever higher.
Each breath ye take swings galaxies wide,
Thy ribs arching as spiral arms beside.

When your steps press on the yielding ground,
Comets and pillars move without sound;
Ancient ice bears thy journey along,
To rhythms older than any mortal song.
When beauty enchants with a cunning gleam,
Seek thy star that burns through the dream.

This body, the dust, a vessel untrue,
This mind but a shadow unreal passing through;

No anchor it holds in the sky of Thine,
Yet the star within is the gift of Thine.
It outshines suns that may collapse in despair,
A spark of blaze wisely hidden there.

And when the hour arrives, veiled and still,
The frame shall dissolve by Thy higher will;
Yet the lamp shall rise beyond the night,
Breaking the veil with its timeless flight.
It joins the chorus of orbs on high,
That sing since dawns before dawn lit the sky.

So walk in silence, yet walk in flame,
Bearing the hidden, unspoken Name;
The star in the skeleton, fierce yet mild,
A secret crown for the Thy own child.
In dust you wander, in light you reign,
Eternal is Thy spark no death can chain.

120

The Unseen Occupant

Seek, and ye shall find the way,
This vessel of flesh is not to stay.
A robe that hangs, yet does not bind,
Though tongues proclaim it our own kind.
A traveller destined for dust or flight,
While all abide in unseen light.

The mind, a whirlwind of joy and pain,
A painted garden in sun and rain;
Its visions vivid, yet its storms deceive,
And dreamers forget the dreams they weave.
Yet all must bow to the eternal existence,
Where even mighty globes find peace at ease.

The path not too calm, yet the road to truth,
Lies scattered in fragments hidden from view.
Few will bend to gather each shard,
Most clutch at shadows, mistaking the guard.
A reflection chased will never be the Sun,
Until the soul beholds the whole as one.

Look instead to truth, not carved but clear,
In birds that fly and the mountains near.

In the silent lamp the soul ignites,
A flame untouched by days or nights.
These illusions fade, and the wise shall ascend,
Walking uncloaked where the stars extend.

There the Atman moves, yet body fades,
Beyond all names, beyond all shades.
A spark within, a secret star,
Illumined, free, in Thy own care.
And the unseen occupant takes its flight,
Re-merging with the vast, eternal Light.

121

In Bloom & Fade, the Truth is Made

In bloom and fade, the truth is shown,
A secret seed the Heart has sown.
My garden weaves a fragrant crown,
The Golden Champak drifting down;
From tender buds that dare to rise,
To blossoms gazing at boundless skies.

Their perfume floats on the softened air,
Wooing clever hearts to linger there.
Some in youth with a trust in divine,
Some in splendour's golden shine.
Each petal whispers what time must prove,
That 'fading is but the path to Love'.

Some bow low as dusk draws near,
As returning dust to dust, all sincere.
Their silent fall, their flashy stay,
Proclaims that all must yield one day.
Yet through their song, my soul hast stirred:
"All life belongs to Thee, O' world."

But man, unheeding, turns aside,
Blind to the truth in bloom's decline.
He clings to form, forgets the breath,
And trembles at the thought of death.
Till by the Manasa Sarovar's tranquil shore,
He learns Thy grace, and fears no more.

There mirrored waters still and deep,
Awakening the soul from mortal sleep;
The Champak's crown, both bloom and dust,
Restores in man a sacred trust,
That through all fading, one flame remains,
A fragrance eternal the heart retains.

122

The Lamp Beyond Bloom and Fade

A few days passed, the Champak swayed,
Its blossoms gold, its buds arrayed;
The flowers shone as once before,
Yet my wonder saw something more.
Old buds to blossoms, and flowers fade,
New buds arise where death is laid;
Thus life repeats in circling rings,
And aids decay to crown new kings.

The old bows low, its colours fade,
While newborn buds their shine have made;
For every leaf that drifts away,
A greener song begins to play.
Thus life renews in silent grace,
And time yields space for time to trace;
The fading leaf, the rising bloom,
One breath dispels both birth and tomb.

Upon the near banana's grace,
A squirrel came with furtive pace;
It sought the nectar's fragrant stream,

A thirst to sate before the day's gleam.
It stripped away the withered bloom,
But found no sweetness to consume;
And so it leapt from branch to bough,
In hope some hidden flower would allow.

And is not man the same at dawn,
When night's long veil is nearly gone?
He seeks Thy nectar pure and bright,
To fill his soul with morning light.
Yet if the draught is not bestowed,
He turns to paths where shadows go;
Unknowing still, it's all Thy play,
That leads ye from night to day.

And when at last the circle breaks,
The soul from fleeting bloom awakes;
It drinks the draught no death can dry,
The nectar poured from realms on high.
And its crown no longer fades to dust,
Its light no longer bends to rust;
But shining still, it soars above,
A circle sealed in endless love.

123

The soul behind bars

Caged parrots, perhaps are our souls confined,
By ego's bars, by the will of mind;
Fed on the seeds of fleeting desire,
Blind to the sky and its endless choir.

They mimic the songs the world imparts,
Echoes of shadows on the borrowed hearts;
Yet deep within, a hunger remains,
For wings unchained, for boundless skies.

Bright wings are folded in silent ache,
Dreaming of streams they've yet to wake;
They wait for the faith that splits the bars,
For a dawn to reveal their native stars.

Then if swiftly the cage bursts apart,
And the sky pours in like a living heart;
The chains grow weak, the feathers flame,
And souls ascend where none can claim.

For no cage binds what was born for flight,
No prison veils the eternal Light;
The spirit flows in its cosmic stream,
Returning home from the cage of dream.

124

Rain, Thy Blissful Bain

The rain, whence Thy blessing gently pours,
Unasked, it knocks on all the silent doors;
Each soul receives in the hour decreed,
That none shall thirst, nor suffer need.

Thy streams descend in secret ways,
Unseen by eyes, yet crowned with praise;
As silver whispers in tender fall,
That cradle the roots, to nourish all.

Some sink deep to the hidden veins,
Some wander forth in crystal chains;
Some join the river's laughing flight,
While some lie still in the lap of night.

So moves the path of mortal breath,
Through veils of life, through gates of death;
Blessings arrive though veiled from sight,
Guiding the feet through the shifting night.

Better a gift that waits its day,
Than one too soon to fade away;
For Thy will, both sure and true,
Brings rain and grace when they are due.

And when the last clouds gently cease,
The soul shall wake in fields of peace;
Bathed in the rain no drought can bind,
Thy blissful stream of eternal bond.

125

The Breath Unseen

Thy air surrounds both land and sea,
A gift so worthy, unseen, and endlessly;
No root can grow, no heart can stay,
Without Thy breath to guide the way.

Each rise and fall of mortal breast,
Is lulled within Thy tender rest;
Yet seldom thanks, and fewer see,
The depth of Thy vast charity.

Through noisy streets, through restless chase,
Ye trade Thy calm for passing pace;
And ye miss the hymn Thy breezes sing,
That stirs the dawn on its silent wing.

The air, the thread of mortal span,
The equal gift to beast and man;
Its mercy wide, its freedom vast,
Beyond the first and the final breath, all cast.

Awake, O' man, to what ye breathe,
Before the day takes its leave;
Each breath is more than lust or fame,
It speaks of Thee, Who none can name.

So harm no life for selfish claim,
But guard the sky, the wind and the flame;
Let forests rise, let rivers flow, that all may grow,
That all may breathe, and life may glow.

For when each breath with others shares,
And joins the song that heaven bears;
The earth shall sing, the sky shall care,
And peace shall float on every breath of air.

And when the final breath is freed,
It blends with Thine, the Source, the Seed;
No cage remains, no fear, no strife,
But only Thee, the breath of Life.

126

Metanoia of The Elements

Let the earth quake in trembling awe,
As heaven cleaves in shards of fire and light;
Let seas roar themselves with foaming rage,
And hurl their roaring psalms into the night.

Let rain descend in mad cascade,
Each drop a spear, each stream so wide;
Let mountains pour their milk of stone,
As if to chisel anew what Thee hast sown.

Let the breath of the world turn tempest,
And storm through valleys like kings restored;
Let willows weep, and sequoias groan,
Their roots laid bare, in truth ignored.

The grasses weep their silver balm,
Soft dew for pilgrims who pass in haste;
Yet who shall bend to taste its calm,
When blinded by the fevered race?

Let earth bestow both thorn and rose,
Each ordained as the eternal knows;
For in the thorn a crown is made,
And in the rose Thy grace displayed.

And every soul, a wanderer lone,
Shall mount the cloud no foot has known;
A pilgrim sailing paths unmarked,
Beyond return, beyond the dark.

There in the turning of all things,
In the fearless stride through untraced skies,
Awaits the wondrous metanoia,
Where self is lost, and Truth shall rise.

127

One Earth, One Race, One Soul

Children are cast into a restless race,
The chase of shadows, the race of haste;
Nameless dreams are pressed into their minds,
"To strive, to conquer, to own the lands."

But poison drips as a hidden seed,
Draining the spirit with selfish greed;
Life is bent from its rightful way,
Chased by the whip, with no delay.

Round and round the oxen tread,
In circles of sorrow, the ages bleed;
False fires blaze on hills of lies,
While truth lies bound, and the spirit cries.

All they gather shall crumble to dust,
For dust is the fate of flesh they trust;
Death shall knock with an unseen hand,
Stripping the false of its borrowed stand.

The heart still trembles with peace's tone,
The note of love it has always been known.

But none will listen, for all would prove,
Their fleeting power, their shadowed groove.

O' world, the bridge of unity stands near,
Yet we build high walls of doubt and fear;
One gentle word could bind all hands and lands,
Yet fighting scatters land in shifting hands.

Division claws where love should grow,
It seeds the frost, it steals the glow;
But unity blooms in a single embrace,
And shower the earth with a brighter face.

Ash shall rain on the final field,
Egos shattered, no sword to wield.
The Earth shall weep in voiceless pain,
For a selfish war that leaves any seed to gain.

Still, skies whisper, the forests sing,
The stars bear witness of everything;
They murmur softly in night's deep scroll:
"One Earth, One Race, One Soul."

For seas divide, yet seas unite,
Their depths conceal, as their waves invite;
And all who breathe, who walk, who climb,
Are threads of Thy eternal rhyme.

The mountains hold their ancient stone,
A truth the ages have always known:
No border, no nation, no luring throne,
The earth was never one's alone.

But if the soul awakens whole,
As One Earth, One Race, One Soul,
If truth is planted where lies have grown,
The inner Light shall make itself known.

Then wisdom shines like a sudden flame,
Peace shall crown the earth again;
As an instant that shines in a blaze untamed,
Never before, and never again as destined.

And when at last all wars are still,
And all hearts surrender to Thy own will,
The song of Thee shall kiss the whole:
One Earth, One Race, One Soul.

128

The Breath Beyond Gold

All strive and toil with hurried breath,
As though to outrun time and death;
Yet few will pause with inward sight,
To glimpse the path of truth and light.

Eight decades long a span may seem,
Yet days slip past as but a dream;
The wheel of seasons turns its face,
And none may halt its silent pace.

Men chase the gold, the fleeting store,
As though they'd reign forevermore;
A thousand coins may decorate the day,
Yet dust shall claim them all one day.

They crave far more than hearts allow,
Yet more comfort shall bloom a century from now;
And what we build with sweat and care,
Shall echo as laughter a century there.

The thrones of men are dust of tomorrow,
As joy turns rust, and hope to sorrow;
What shines today in time decays,
The wheel keeps turning through its maze.

Yet bread for the hungry, water to share,
Outlive the palaces built on despair;
For love is the coin no moth defiles,
The wealth of the soul, the treasure worthwhile.

Though kings may reap their dreaming gain,
Amass their hoards, extend their chain;
Their years, though prized, are but a breath,
Numbered, measured, and sealed by death.

What if, instead of hollow greed,
We sought the heart, the simple need?
The child would feast, the poor would rise,
And none go hungry beneath the skies.

But greed, the phantom, blinds the eyes,
It whispers wealth, it weaves its lies;
Men fight for shadows they cannot claim,
And wake to sorrow, loss, and shame.

The ocean groans with restless tide,
While dreamers drift, unmoored aside;
They sleep through days the heavens give,
And walk awake, yet cease to live.

Why hoard what moth and rust consume?
Why build on sand that grants no room?
The riches kept for selfish aim,
Shall burn to ashes in the flame.

Still man must strive, for so he's made,
To labour on till the light shall fade;

Yet let that labour sow Thy seed,
Not to feed the barren roots of greed.

For sloth bears fruit of withered pain,
A heavy yoke, a wasted chain;
But labour free, with love to guide,
Shall taste the joy that will abide.

So learn, O' soul, the higher worth,
Forsake the mirage of owning earth;
For life abides not in wealth or fame,
But in Thy breath from which it came.

129

The Sea of Thee

O Breath of the unseen, so still, so free,
Thou movest through all, yet none may see;
O Cradle of seed ere it dares to rise,
O Stir of the tides 'neath the watching skies.

In silence, Thou art the pulse that stays;
In motion, Thou art the hidden base.
In the fire's blaze, Thou art the cool of the flame,
In winter's depth, Thou art the rule without name.

No hand can hold Thy eternal face,
Yet hearts that listen shall know that grace;
A Voice unheard, older than star or flame,
Its script is written in the season's name.

The earth a wheel, and the sun its steed,
The galaxies drift as lanterns freed;
Numberless suns in Thy glorious ride,
Each one afloat in Thy boundless tide.

Our days are but whispers, our years but breath,
Yet Thou dost guide us through life and death;
The same bright Vibe that makes stars burn,
Shall flame within us, and the flame shall return.

When veils are lifted and mists depart,
The breath becomes a hymn in the seeker's heart;
No longer he chases the shores above,
For the Ocean dwells within is eternal love.

Shadows shall bow and the chains shall break,
The sage shall drink from the hidden lake;
The desert shall bloom with the spring's release,
And the lost heart be crowned with nirvana's peace.

Blessed are the eyes that no longer strive,
Blessed are the ears where Thy music is alive;
For Truth walks naked through time and space,
Clothed in the light of the tender grace.

O Lord, Thy Love is a sea without seam,
The wave that carries each whispered dream;
Its song is the play of Thy hidden fire,
It's depth, the home of the soul's desire.

The stars may wither, the suns may fall,
But Thy vast current upholds them all;
Time is a ripple upon Thy shore,
Yet Thy deep silence abides evermore.

All flames return to Thy eternal Light,
All rivers return to Thy boundless sea;
And every pilgrim, through night or day,
Finds the Love, the Truth, the Way.

No crown shall remain, no throne shall stay,
All kingdoms crumble, all dust decays;

Yet Love shall reign when the worlds are gone,
For Love is the Sea we are drifting upon.

O the Depth beyond words, O the Height unseen,
Thy face is the light in all that has been;
Through shadows of ages Thy whisper calls,
The Sea of Thee breaks down every wall.

And when the end of all paths shall be,
There awaits no shore but the Sea of Thee;
No wave nor ripples divided, no self apart,
The drop is the Ocean, the ocean Thy heart.

130

Into the sea of Thee

Before the first dawn cracked the silence,
An Emptiness moved - no edge, no guidance,
Only the trembling, vibes of the endless Being,
A pulse unseen, and a still seeing.

In that boundless tide, the galaxies bloomed,
Trillions of sparks in darkness groomed;
Each lantern cradled a billion suns,
Each sun its worlds, in their whirls and runs,
Each world a stage for life's small flame,
A tiny spark without a name.

Somewhere, half-hidden in the milky way,
Our world spins, unseen by any day;
Faster than a hawk, swifter than a dart,
Yielding to its own rhythmic heart;
And upon that sphere, a creature stands,
Made of dust, building kingdoms and lands.

It names the oceans, counts the skies,
Dreams itself the centre wise;
Never seeing the inside bliss,
Though in Thy boundless bless.

The Almighty speaks in light-years wide,
In comet's sweep, in nebulae's tide,
Mountains as motes, empires as air,
A single life, a breathless prayer.
That bends to lift the sparrow's fall,
Counts the hairs of all and caress all.

Such is the paradox we meet,
That we are nothing, yet complete;
In Thy gaze, all things reside,
The micro and macro side by side.

So let the measure of the cosmos be,
The gauge of awe in you and me;
And let the measure of Thy mercy true,
Be the truth and trust we hold in all we do;
Until we fall back to the Breath we claim,
Returning home, unnamed, aflame.

Each star, each spark, each trembling ray,
Moves within Thy vast, unbroken sway;
The rays of light, the tides of time,
Flow towards the Source, eternal, prime.
All voyages end where all beginnings hide,
Where every wave and wind abide.

The skies collapse, the comets flee,
Yet Thy deep current holds them free;
The smallest breath, the longest year,
All an echo in Thy presence clear.

O' the Soul of souls, O' the boundless Sea,
All flows return, all things to Thee.

The winds shall whisper, the oceans sing,
The mountains bow, the valleys bring;
All life unites in Thy embrace,
Each soul dissolves, no trace, no space.
And we, the sparks, shall merge and see,
The infinite Heart of the Sea of Thee.

131

The Whisper of Eternal Light

The earth may turn, the stars may flame,
Yet still I rest beneath Thy name;
Through passing clouds, through cries of night,
A silence guards with Thy hidden light.

The river bends, the forest sighs,
Each life returns, each shadow dies;
The passing breath, the veil of dream,
Dissolves into Thy boundless stream.

The mind may weave a thousand snares,
The heart may chase its gilded cares;
Yet all are but reflections pale,
Of Thy pure flame that shall prevail.

The moments slip like grains of sand,
Through grasping thought, through mortal mind;
Desires may rise, then break and fall,
Yet none escape Thy ocean's call.

Ye dream of dawns, lament the past,
Surmising breath alone shall ever last;

The clock may chime, the hours deceive,
Yet the truth abides where none may grieve.

The body wanes, the senses tire,
The soul burns on with hidden fire;
Through veils of night the wise shall see,
The dawn of Light that sets them free.

Beneath the weight of passing years,
I walk through fields of hopes and fears;
The path is narrow, yet stars still guide,
Though pride would draw my steps aside.

I drank of wells that promised cheer,
Yet found them empty, tangled, drear;
For only in Thy silent spring I find,
The waters pure that heal my mind.

The voices rise like a restless tide,
They paint the false, they mask the pride;
But in the hush of holy night,
I hear Thy whisper emitting light.

132

Walking Past the Edge of Light

Seek to find, ye soul of flame,
Not for an echo, not for fame.
The world is lost in endless quest,
Yet truth is found in the inward rest.

Knock, and the hidden door shall rise,
A dawn unveiled before thy eyes.
But if the mind forgets the goal,
The night shall bind the wandering soul.

The seeker walks through year on years,
Through fleeting joy and passing tears.
Yet when the pearl of Light is won,
The searching fades, the work is done.

Read not the scroll for lore alone,
Nor cling to words as a carven stone.
For if the word awakens Thy sight,
The book is sealed, the soul takes flight.

But those who thirst and find no wine,
Shall walk again through time's design.

Yet ye descendants seek, ye children pray,
Through countless nights, through dawning days.

Seek not as others bid ye go,
Their map is dust, their guide is shadow.
Seek not the path that crowds commend,
The way is thine, thine own to the end.

The towers of mind shall crack and fall,
The flesh shall fail, the gold shall pall.
Yet love endures, a ceaseless flame,
The source, the root, Thy hidden name.

The narrow gate no hand may bind,
It yields to hearts by truth refined.
No pride may pass, no greed may stay,
The meek shall walk the timeless way.

Seek not the shadow, seek Thy fire,
The still small whisper, the only desire.
For there the restless tides are stilled,
And every hope of man fulfilled.

What gain in seeking, if not found?
What worth in a song without the sound?
But the one who finds, no more shall roam,
His soul shall join the still at Home.

Thus ends the chase, the endless race,
The seeker drowned in boundless grace.
No two remain, no walls, no cord,
The seeking ends, behold the Thy chord.

And in that hush, all cries are stilled,
The will dissolved, and Thy law fulfilled.
The Sea receives the drop once free,
The drop becomes eternity.

133

Epilogue – The Return to The Vastness

In words too frail for such endless weight,
I reach towards the nameless gate,
The pulse unseen, the vibe untold,
That binds the dust to stars of gold.

From stone to flame, from void to sea,
All turns within Thy endless harmony;
Before the dawn of time's first breath,
Thou unseen, unshaken by life or death.

The earth spins so swift, the hawk outflown,
Yet not by strength, nor a power of its own;
It rides on Thy current, vast, unseen,
Upon a stream where all worlds convene.

The sun, a pilgrim crowned with fire,
Moves through Thy tide that has no shire;
While galaxies beyond all names and fame,
Sail on Thy sea, both wild but tame.

At light's swift pace the moon is near,
The sun but moments from our sphere;

Yet to the Milky galaxy's veiled rim,
Five hundred thousand years grow so dim.

And farther still, the endless wisdoms spread,
Where time is born and time lies dead;
Where space itself dissolves away,
And night gives birth to a brighter day.

O' alpha the veiled, O' omega the bright,
Where zero clasps at infinity's height;
Thy shape is silence, vast, profound,
Yet every atom is Thy own sound.

I am but dust, a fleeting flame,
A shadow clothed in borrowed name;
Yet graced to breathe, to stand, to see,
Within Thy boundless mystery.

The little known no tongue can tell,
The greater still no brain may spell;
Yet all is kept in Thy embrace,
The unfailing love, the unmeasured grace.

So hear the spin, the rushing spheres,
The wheel that turns beyond the years;
Let thirst for shores at last be stilled,
And hearts with Thy holy voyage fulfilled.

Till comes the hour, serene, untrod,
When self dissolves in Thee, O' Lord;
No crown, no name, no voice, no call,
The ocean swallows this drop and all.

And in that final, holy tide,
No I remains, no Thou to hide;
But only Thy vastness, calm, complete,
In the quiet Heart, where all shall meet.

Now, nothing more shall my pen breathe,
Until Thy mercy parts the heavens once more
And lets the golden rays descend down in grace.